I'M DONE.

Praise for

LUCY SHAHJAHAN

"Thank you, Lucy, for this life-changing program. Everything about it spoke directly to my heart, especially the tough love. You don't let us have excuses, you keep us accountable and you don't take our shit. But you also come from a completely loving place and want the best for us. You build us up so we feel empowered to change our lives.

Every part of your program is carefully planned and designed so we come out of it feeling like completely authentic versions of ourselves who are empowered to create anything we want."

-KATE H.

Lucy is a fucking rockstar Queen who will support you, push you and help you to see your true beauty. If you want to come into more of your true essence, Lucy can help you to get there.

- AUDREY M

"You can tell Lucy's passionate about what she does - she has everyone's back, and her energy and light are contagious. She genuinely cares about the women in her program.

Plus, she's very intuitive. I seriously felt like she had a crystal ball or had tapped my phone, because every time I struggled with something, she'd post a video saying exactly what I needed to hear.

You can tell she walks the walk, and she knows what she's talking about because she's gone through the process herself.

- ZULLY P

Lucy is the most truthful, no-BS person I've ever known. She's an incredible coach and mentor who won't let you slack off. I love her uplifting energy and authenticity. She really cares and delivers great results.

- MEI W

Soul to Soul is like no other program out there. It's all about opening your heart, deeply connecting with who you truly are, and having unconditional love for yourself. When you know who you are, you know what you want, and life becomes truly phenomenal.
Lucy is like a best friend who holds you to your highest, and calls you out on the limiting beliefs and old stories that have kept you small and stuck for so long. She's your biggest advocate for self-love, self-worth and how it's possible to create the future you dream of.

- KATE T

Acknowledgements

To my incredible husband, Anaam, for holding such a huge space for me with everything that I do. You are an outstanding father, son, husband and man in the world. You backed me all the way with this book and encouraged me to keep going on the days when the process started to lag. You are my oak tree, and I am grateful for you every day.

To my divine daughter, Abella, for coming into our lives. She was in my tummy when I spoke this book into existence, and in the world when I was bringing the book to life. Thank you for teaching me what love is every single day. It is an honor to be your mama, and I treasure you with every fiber of my being.

To my dad for supporting me from the sidelines in heaven. Losing him has taught me so much and put me on this path of self-discovery.

To my amazing mum, who has supported me and always given me the freedom to do what I need to do in the world. I love you.

To my gorgeous brother, Dave, who has always been in my corner, cheering me on from the sidelines and believing in me.

To my fairy godmother, Rebecca Anuwen. Thank you for your unwavering support with this book and in life. You are a gift, and I am so grateful to call you a soul sister.

To Dorothy Fraser, thank you for holding me to my highest, always. You are a rare diamond, and I value you deeply.

To my rockstar editing team for holding huge space for me with this book. Thank you for a dream collaboration, and for getting me right out of the gate! I appreciate you coming into my life to make this book into the book it needed to be for so many women.

To my amazing assistant, Charlotte Barnes, for being such an incredible support to me. I can count on you always. Thank you for jumping on whatever needed to be done to help make this book process easier. You are a gem!

To my gorgeous dog, Stevie Nicks - thank you for all the cuddles and support when I needed them most. You are the best dog a girl could have, and you bring so much joy to my life.

Finally, thank you to all my phenomenal sisters who've done my program, *Soul to Soul* and chosen themselves fully. You each make this world a better place by being ALL of you, and every one of you inspired me along the way. You are a huge source of inspiration to get this book into the world so we can keep on rising and supporting each other collectively.

Dedication

This book was a download from the
Divine and it flowed through my soul.

I dedicate it to you as an epic woman
who's ready to claim her full feminine
power, open her heart and walk in her
own glorious, potent energy. I see you,
I am you and I love you. You deserve a
soulmate relationship, and having love in
your life is your birthright.

May we raise the vibration on this planet
together, living in our abundance with
love as our currency.

TABLE OF CONTENTS

I'M DONE.

Hello, divine woman!

Hello divine woman! I'm so happy that you are *done* because it's only from this place that we can truly open ourselves up to something new that can put us on our path.

When I was finally *done*, I discovered something profound that changed the trajectory of my life. That was my Vortex and I can't wait to share more about that later.

My name is Lucy Shahjahan, and it's my absolute honor to share everything I've learned, and everything I teach my clients, with you here in this book.

Firstly, I want to let you know that I used to suck at love and relationships. I used to always give my power away. I put men on pedestals. Thank *God* I did the work to change that shitshow I was living in. And now I'm so excited that I get to share with you how I changed my life, and how you can too.

I know you're here because, on the surface, everything is fantastic... But I also know that if we scratch beneath the jazz hands, it's a whole different story, isn't it? I know you once had a dream to be married, or at least be in a very committed relationship with the love of your life. And if you're like a lot of women, that dream also included becoming a mum.

But somewhere along the way, that bright, sparkly dream got dimmer and dimmer. And now, deep down, you've given up on believing that it can ever actually happen for you.

You're so fucking *over* men not making you the priority. In fact, if you're honest, you don't trust men or love any more. Maybe you've started to wonder whether you just weren't meant to have a soulmate relationship? Maybe you're just meant to be an aunty in this life? What's even scarier is that you've now convinced yourself that that would be enough for you.

Because, look, you've done vision boards, read self-help books and listened to so many podcasts that you've literally lost count of them. You do regular yoga, and meditate when you can... but you're still wondering where the fuck this perfect man is.
It perplexes you that he hasn't shown up yet. I mean you have good friends, you're beautiful and you're a good person. So why the hell is it taking so damn long?

This is not what you signed up for!

Not only that, but you're also pissed off that all your friends seem to attract their perfect guys. Why does it have to be so freaking hard for you? The only logical explanation is that the Universe must play favorites!

Meanwhile, if you have to go to one more baby shower or engagement party as the only single friend left standing, you're gonna punch yourself in the face. This 'feeling left behind' energy is beginning to show up in other places too. You've been meaning to start your own business, or get that promotion, or find a completely new job... but the sense of imposter syndrome keeps holding you back and you're *terrified* to fail.

Sister, I FEEL you.

I've been where you are, and I'm here to tell you that shit is about to get REAL. And your life? It's about to get pretty fucking epic.
But. Before you do anything else, right now, in this moment, I want you to commit 100% to being an open vessel and really receive the information in this book. I can't do all the heavy lifting as you read. So can I count on you to bring yourself to the party, and let yourself truly take it all in?

Because, let me tell you, if you can't? There's literally no point in you reading this. You have to be done with getting in your own way. You have to be ready to align with your own epic-ness. You can absolutely learn how to attract your King - but the catch is that you have to bring your A-game.

Working through this book is a co-creation. Think of me as your new partner in crime. But, like with any good partnership, you have to work with me and do your bit as you read. Otherwise, you're better off just bingeing on Netflix, keeping yourself busy and continuing to build your life solo.

Are you with me?

OK then, let's do this! So. I want you to start by sitting somewhere comfy. Close your eyes, then put your right hand on your heart and your left hand on your belly. Take a moment to just feel that beautiful connection with yourself.

As you move out of your head and into this moment in your body, you'll be able to receive whatever it is that you truly need. And, as you connect with your heart, I also want you to breathe in the energy of accepting that you're *exactly* where you're supposed to be.

Know that this book is for you. Know that it has the potential to completely crack open your worldview and the way that you see yourself. Know that it can utterly transform the way you relate to love, relationships, men and - honestly - the entire world around you.

Now, take a big breath in and release.

Nice work.

Beauty, this is your invitation. I want you to feel deep into your heart. You've been put on this planet because you are absolutely magnificent. You are whole and complete. You are a fucking gift to this world. And it's your birthright to have a soulmate relationship, along with everything else that you desire. Full. Stop.

I know that feels like a lot to take in - but stay with me and let it sink in.

That's the very first thing I want you to hear. I want you to know it.
I want you to feel it. I want you to connect deeply with that reality.
Because the ONLY reason I'm writing this book is that I want to put
an end to the suffering you experience daily. I want to kick this 'not-
enough-ness' right to the curb. These patterns, these behaviors, these
thoughts you have? They're keeping you separated from your divine
light, from your divinity and from your life's purpose.

I speak to way too many beautiful, intelligent women who are just like
you. They come from all around the world, but deep down, they share a
feeling of being undeserving in their core. They describe it as a heavy
ball of sadness in the pits of their stomachs.

So right now, let yourself connect to those feelings. Connect with
where they live in your body. Connect with how you actually feel about
yourself and about love. That feeling that, no matter what you do, love
just never happens for you. You don't feel worthy of it. Regardless of
how hard you try, you just keep attracting the same guy with a different
name and nothing ever goes anywhere.

Maybe something happened to you as a little girl. Maybe life has dealt
you some shitty cards. Either way, deep down, you gave up a long time
ago, and now you're stuck in the story that love just doesn't work out
for you.

Well, guess what? I'm here to say to you that that's *bullshit*.

You CAN absolutely have love in your life.

I'm living proof.

For so many years, I was that woman who felt she completely didn't
deserve love. I created a mindblowing number of coping mechanisms
for it - waiting for that next drink, hanging out with friends, partying
in an attempt to forget that I wasn't actually happy. I was stuck in the
story of being undeserving, and all those coping mechanisms did a
great job of keeping me from seeing just how unhappy I truly was.

Meanwhile, I stayed busy outsourcing my inner work - going to healers,

kinesiologists and psychics, or talking with friends. Really though, I was just outsourcing, outsourcing, outsourcing. I can't tell you how much money was going out - I just wanted to get it fixed and I wanted someone to do it for me!
But after all that 'work', my heart was still closed.

Thank God I woke the fuck up, and made the decision to do whatever it took to get out of my own way and open up my heart. Because just three months after I did, I met my now-husband in New York City, of all places. You know, the city that's labeled as 'hard to meet anyone in'? Yep, that's where I met him.

It happened because I cleaned up my mindset, and finally opened up to the idea of love happening for me without a shadow of doubt. I made a bold declaration to the Universe that I was ready for him to come into my life, then I asked it to do the heavy lifting.
I went offline because dating apps no longer felt aligned, and I told the Universe, "I'll say yes to every invitation you send my way." (To be clear, there weren't many at that point. I was so entrenched in rehearsing for the off-Broadway show I was working on and waitressing to earn a living that I barely even had a life!)

Sure enough, though, I met this lovely Indian woman on the set of a film, and she invited me along to her birthday drinks.
When her birthday swung around, going was the last thing I felt like doing. It was in a trendy bar all the way uptown, it was a freezing winter night and it was raining. I'd just finished work at midnight, and I thought, *"Urghhh, am I seriously going to schlepp uptown to an Indian party where I know no one? I barely even know the birthday girl!"* But I held strong in my pact with the Universe, and uptown I went.

I watched the taxi meter ticking over as we sat in standstill traffic and thought, *"This is ridiculous. I'm not going to meet my soulmate there anyway. It's an Indian drinks party. Indian men just aren't my type."*
Then, when I got to the party, there was a huge queue. So I marched up to the bouncer and said, "Listen, I'm not waiting in this line. You're going to let me in. I'm going inside to a party where I know no one. I'm pretty sure the love of my life isn't here, so I'll be here for 15 minutes max. Please, just let me in!"

I think he was quite scared of me, so he let me go through.
And surprise, surprise, it turns out that my soulmate was in there. Just as I was leaving, the birthday girl introduced me to a guy called Anaam.

I thought to myself, *"What kind of name is THAT?"* but said hello to him. We talked briefly, and in our conversation, he admitted that he was completely done with the corporate world but hadn't left it yet. Being me, I cut straight to the chase and grilled him on why he wasn't living on purpose.

He replied that I was quite intense and needed to chill out. I agreed, and said I needed to go bed - explaining that I was playing Hillary Clinton in a one-woman show and that I was exhausted. I left soon after that without giving him my number, but he found me on Facebook and asked me out on a date.

Initially, I wasn't interested. I figured that if he was the kind of guy to play it safe and just reach out over Facebook, he didn't stand a chance with me. I'll get to the best bits of our story later in the book, but for now, I'll just say that despite this, yep, we went out together.

In the leadup to the date, I still didn't think he was my type... but something about his calm energy got me curious. And I'm so glad I was curious, because I knew on that date that he was exactly who I'd been calling in. I felt it in our hug. I hugged this guy like a cling bear - hard enough that he asked me if I was OK - LOL!

I said that I *clearly* needed a good hug, and I told him that he had very good arms and was very huggable.

We've been together ever since. Fast forward to now, and we have a beautiful little girl together and a divine Aussie shepherd dog called Stevie Nicks. Baby No.2 is in the wings and we can't wait to expand our family.

It's the life I used to dream of. And now it's my reality.

I want to let you in on the secret that made this dream become my reality: I got to know my Vortex, and I learned how to use it. What's a Vortex? It's your main tool for creating the life you desire. Everything that happens to you happens first in your Vortex. It's the energy field that you create in. If you create shit in your Vortex, you'll live shit. If you create the life of your dreams in there, you'll start to live the life of your dreams.

Once I started to understand how my Vortex worked, I began to create a deeper connection with my heart each day. As I did, I found that the more time I spent feeling grateful for the future I wanted to manifest, the faster that future happened. Feeling gratitude in every fiber of your being **in advance** for what you're calling in is one of the most powerful ways to create it. So I started to consciously spend more time in this sacred space, this Vortex of creative energy.

And, as I mentioned above, it WORKED.

I like to call the form of gratitude I started to use 'the supersonic, 3D version of gratitude'. It's like gratitude on steroids. Feeling that kind of gratitude - breathing it and living it - will change your life, and fast.

Then, once I really understood my Vortex and how to use it, I became unstoppable. My life changed so much, so fast, and it was AMAZING.

In this book, you'll discover more about what your Vortex is, its purpose, and how to use it to attract your soulmate and the life of your dreams. You'll learn how and why you've been sabotaging yourself, and what to do about it. And along the way, you'll develop rockstar boundaries, keep your vibration high, drop your 'love armor', and finally learn how to be 100% of your own, vulnerable, unapologetic, epic self.

But to make that happen, you first need to accept one thing.

You need to accept that YOU are the one who creates change in your life, and you need to accept it *now*. It's not the drugs or alcohol or food that you're relying on. It's not the friends that you're venting to. It's not even the therapist that you're just regurgitating the same old crap to. You are the creator of your life, so you have to want to live your best life, right now.

I'M DONE.

That's why, before we dive any further into this book, I want you to choose to accept this fully. There can't be any, "*I hope this works,*" or committing halfway. That's why you are where you are at the moment. You have to be all in and TRUST in the process fully for it to work for you.

Can I count on you to do that?

Yes?

OK, fabulous. Let's do this.

Let's get into your Vortex!

A NOTE ABOUT THIS BOOK

Most of the women I work with are straight and looking for their soulmate relationship with a man. That doesn't mean that I think this is what all relationships should look like. I acknowledge that there's a full spectrum of relationship types out there, and I respect and value all of them.

However, the language in this book reflects the women I work with. If you are an LGBTQIA+ woman and you're looking for a soulmate relationship with someone who isn't a man, you may still get a lot out of this book. You'll just have to change the language in your head as you read.

(And if you're not looking for a soulmate relationship at all, then this probably isn't the book for you.)

Additionally, to maintain privacy and confidentiality, and keep my community a safe, powerful, sacred space, all names in the client stories have been changed.

CHAPTER ONE

What exactly is

THE VORTEX?

"You are held by the Universe"

So what, exactly, is your Vortex? In short, it's a portal that you can use to create the life of your dreams - and create it from your heart.

You see, whether you know it or not, you're creating in your Vortex 100% of the time. So before we go any deeper into how your Vortex works (and how to work with it), it's worth taking some time now to really understand it at a heart level.

WHAT IS THE VORTEX

I first heard the term 'the Vortex' from Esther Hicks. (And, as a side note, if you've never listened to any of Esther and Jerry Hicks' stuff, I highly recommend it... once you've finished putting everything you learn in THIS book into action, of course! So many of my clients tell me they can understand Esther's work much better after they've worked with me.)

Esther talks about a 'vortex of creation'. But she has her image of what the Vortex looks like, and I have mine. We define it differently, too. You might have your own completely different image by the time you get to the end of the chapter, and that's totally OK.

For now though, I want you to know that HOWEVER you visualize it, your Vortex is a giant energetic container. It specifically operates for you to create and hold your dreams, desires and wishes in. You exist inside of it 24/7, whether you're aware of it or not.

But when you're aware of your Vortex and use it properly, beauty, you can create anything you put your mind to.

Your Vortex is where you set and send out the energetic vibration of what you desire, so it can manifest in your life. What do I mean by 'vibration' there? Put simply, it's how you really feel deep down, and what you truly believe about your desires.

Let's say you're asking for something, but you don't genuinely believe the Universe can bring it to you. All your words and requests to the Universe are redundant if you don't actually believe it can happen. You can't trick the Universe with your words... so until you start building your belief muscle, you'll keep falling short.

Consciously connecting with your Vortex, on the other hand, directly connects you with Source / God / The Universe / Spirit / Creator. That makes it your sacred energetic container with the power to bring you EVERYTHING you desire - so use it wisely. Respect it. Honor it. Guard it.

And whatever you do, don't let anyone shit in it!

Right now, you might not be creating within your Vortex consciously, but trust me: you're still creating in it. And the sooner you become aware of how you're creating inside of it, and how fucking potent it is, the sooner you get to make the call on what it holds. And then? Then, beautiful woman, you get the keys to your own kingdom where you can create anything you want in your life.
Pretty epic, isn't it?

The problem is that most of us aren't taught that we even have a Vortex, let alone that we get to control what does and doesn't go into it. We're not taught to dream - instead, it's drummed into us to be realistic and practical. So, as a result of all that realism and practicality, *we believe that life happens to us, instead of for us.* And instead of living the lives we really, truly want, we live the lives we think we're allowed to live, or the lives other people tell us we should be living.

We live the lives we settle for.

DIDN'T KNOW YOU HAD A VORTEX? JOIN THE CLUB – NEITHER DID I!

If you'd told Lucy of 20 years ago that she had a Vortex - one that she was regularly shitting in, by the way - she wouldn't have had a clue what you were talking about. Back then, I was in a day-to-day grind. I knew there was something more to life, but I couldn't figure out how to make it happen for me.

And meanwhile, I lived a life that just didn't feel like mine. Oh, I *looked* like I was living life to the max. I was going out with my friends, drinking and partying and having So. MUCH. Fun. I stayed incredibly busy... because that's how the external voices that I allowed into my Vortex told me I should be enjoying my life.

But that's not what I wanted at a heart and soul level... And part of the reason I stayed so busy was that if I slowed down, even for an instant, I was scared all my shit would come up and inconvenience me with emotions I didn't know what to do with.

Plus, I was also afraid to hear the voice of my heart, which wanted to connect me with my truth. Listening to that voice would require making big changes to my life, and I was in hiding mode. My heart had so many huge dreams and desires, and my fear made it SO much easier to just stay busy all the time.

So I went out, partied and got hangover after hangover. I did whatever I could to numb the fact that I wasn't where I wanted to be at all, and that I was anything but happy with who I was.

Can you relate to that, divine woman? I know a lot of my clients do when they first start to work with me. They describe life before they discover that they are the Queens of their own Vortexes as being an inescapable daily grind, 24/7. They compare it to living Groundhog Day over and over and over again. And they talk about being in a constant state of fight-or-flight, hopelessness and angst.

(PSA side note: let me just take a moment to acknowledge that if you're dealing with clinical depression or anxiety, this book won't take the place of professional therapy. And if therapy is something that is, or could be, helpful for you, I encourage you to embrace it.

That's because I've personally experienced horrible panic attacks that had me scared to leave my apartment for fear of one coming on. I felt like I couldn't breathe, and it was terrifying. These attacks are real, physical reactions in our bodies, and I want you to know that I don't take them lightly. But I've lived through anxiety bad enough to hijack my life - and I'm happy to share that I managed to release that anxiety once I faced my underlying fears and undealt-with emotions.

So now, if I feel another panic attack coming on, I know it's just scattered energy. It means I'm in my head, and I need to drop back into my heart. And I know how to do that now.)

Meanwhile, other women talk about how, in their pre-Vortex-aware world, they used drugs or alcohol to escape their daily lives. They had no idea that they actually had the power to load their Vortex up with what they truly wanted. They just knew they longed to 'be in the driver's seat of their lives'. And chemically altering their state of consciousness - getting *literally* 'out of their heads' - seemed like the best (and sometimes, the only) option at the time.

Besides, it was just what people did, right?

For me, realizing that I had a Vortex and that I'd been filling it with shit was a turning point in my life. Suddenly, instead of trying to drown out the voice of my heart, I started actively listening to it. I started figuring out what the REAL Lucy wanted to fill her Vortex with. And I promised myself that from that moment on, I'd start to back myself. I'd only allow my OWN dreams, desires, intentions and wishes into my Vortex, and I'd start actively blocking anyone else's access to it.

And let me tell you, beauty, it felt so *fucking liberating!*

I like to imagine my life up until then as a beautiful sailboat, berthed in a safe-but-kind-of-boring harbor marina. That turning point - that moment I made my decision to back myself - was like casting off the ropes that held my boat in place. Suddenly, I was leaving that safe-but-boring harbor behind me, and my life was FINALLY moving in the direction I wanted it to.

I was ready to go off on an adventure, so I headed out into the big, deep sea of the unknown to discover what I was made of.

SPEAKING MY NEW LIFE INTO EXISTENCE

One of the first things I did as I allowed 'my boat to set sail' was to speak all the dreams and desires that I wanted to manifest into existence.

For example, I remember the moment I decided that I wanted to move from my hometown of Sydney, Australia to become an actor in New York. People asked me how I'd manage to get myself the Green Card that let me work in the US.

"Easy," I replied. "I'll win the Green Card lottery." No 'if's. No 'but's. No doubts or 'just in case's. Just me and my complete faith and deep knowing that it was GOING to happen for me, thank you very much. In fact, it was already done and taken care of in my mind. That's why I took bold action to sell my belongings and even my trusty purple Holden Barina that had been so good to me. I was leaning into faith more than I ever had before, and it felt fantastic!

*A great quote I love that really speaks to this decision is "**Build it and they will come.**"*

I built the result of moving country so strongly in my mind that everything fell into place, and it absolutely came.

So let me tell you that when my Green Card came through, everyone around me was super-surprised except for me. On some level, I'd known from the moment I'd spoken those words into existence that there could be no other outcome. I truly believed it in my heart, and that's the special ingredient you need to magnetize your desires into your life.

You have to believe with every fiber of your being, no matter what, without the proof in advance.

At the same time though, that moment became a new reference point in my life. Up until then, I'd never been someone who won things. But suddenly, I had clear evidence in the physical world that I could point to and say, "See! I AM someone who wins things. I AM someone good things happen to. And if I can manifest this, I can manifest ANYTHING!"

So right then, I made a sacred vow to never let any other voices into my Vortex to dilute my faith. Not the voice of my mother, not the voices of my friends, and not the voice of society. From that moment on, the only voice I'd allow in was my own.
And every time since then, when resistance has come up or I've found myself scared or thinking negatively, I've reminded myself, "Lucy, just keep putting one foot in front of the other. Just come back to your heart. Keep following through on your heart's desires: they always know the way."

That Green Card was just the first of many of my heart's desires that I spoke into being. I spoke my desire for a great apartment in New York once I arrived, too. Then I spoke my intention to get into the best acting school, and finally – and you'll learn more about this later in the book — I spoke my intention to attract my soulmate.

And one by one, ALL of those desires came into being in my life, fueled by my faith, my imagination and the language I used.

SO, WHAT DOES YOUR VORTEX LOOK LIKE?

As I mentioned at the beginning of this chapter, different women visualize their Vortexes with different imagery. One client imagined hers as a cauldron. If that's too witchy for you, you could think of yours as a giant ocean of possibility (which is how I think of mine). Maybe, if you're more science-inclined, you might see it as an energy field, or a huge room with a magnet at the center. Or, if you're more of a nature child, it might be a beautiful garden where you can plant the sacred-dream-germinating seeds of your desires.

However you want to imagine your Vortex, it's perfect if it makes sense and resonates for you.

The key is that whatever imagery you use, it needs to give you a sense of being a sacred, limitless container that you can create literally ANYTHING you want in. And - more about this later in the book - you do the actual creating simply by asking for what you want.

Then you spend time consciously connecting to your Vortex, seeing and feeling your desire as if it already existed. You fully let in the reality that it exists, and allow yourself to feel that reality deeply on a sensory level in every cell in your body. I used to cry when I visualized my daughter before I became pregnant. The feelings were so real that they brought me to tears, and I could feel my cells rearranging themselves to align with my vision.

I want to be clear here that you can create anything when you're connected to, and paying attention to what you allow into, your Vortex.

Want to create a soulmate? You can do it - and I should know because I did exactly that. Want to create a $500,000+-a-year business? Yep, I did that too. How about a life of traveling the world on a luxury yacht? Put it in your Vortex, then actually do the work in this book, and watch it take shape in ways your everyday, logical mind could never have imagined.

From the outside, creating from your Vortex probably looks like coincidences that keep taking place over and over again. It might look like things just 'happening' to line up for you. Or it might look like insanely good luck or serendipity.

But if you've been working with, and playing in, your Vortex for long enough, you know better. However you decide that your Vortex looks for you, it's the place where you created the circumstances for luck, coincidence and serendipity to manifest.

And when I say preparation, that means working with your imagination consistently, and holding the vision of what you want so strongly that it can't help but happen.

> *"Luck is a matter of preparation*
> *meeting opportunity"*
>
> *–Oprah Winfrey*

BEING PART OF A SISTERHOOD MATTERS!

Let me be crystal clear: the people around you can make or break your Vortex.

Later in this book, I'll go into detail about how to 'feed and care for' your Vortex. We'll talk about how to nurture it, how to protect it, and of course, how to fuel it. For the moment though, I just want to briefly mention the importance of having a community - a positive soul sisterhood - around you as you're connecting with and getting to know your Vortex.

In fact, this is important at any stage of your journey to become the Queen of your own Vortex. But it's ESPECIALLY important now, during the beginning stages.

There are two things I hear over and over again from the women who do my programs or retreats. One is, "Lucy, OMG, I can't BELIEVE how powerful it is to be in a room with a whole circle of women who are supporting my dream. The potency of being here in this group is mindblowing!" And the other - usually a week or two later - is, "Ummmm... Lucy, am I a bad person for suddenly finding it incredibly hard to hang out with my old friends who just want to complain?"

That perfectly illustrates just how much of an impact - both positive and negative - the friends and family you surround yourself with can have on your life. The truth is that none of us can create the lives of our dreams on our own. So you have to be super-selective about who you share your dream with. This was a huge one for me. You won't get to your dream without creating solid boundaries and having the right people supporting you in getting to where you're headed.

Those right people will believe in your dream along with you. They'll reflect it back to you and strengthen your faith in it when you're having an off-day. The wrong people, though? Well, it's a little like - you know when you quit smoking, the first thing they tell you to do is stop hanging around with other smokers? It's exactly the same thing. You're heading off in a new direction, and unless the people you surround yourself with are going the same way, they'll just hold you back.

Otherwise, it's like you're inviting the people around you to pollute your Vortex and poison your dreams. I always think of it as giving those people a free pass to take a dump in that amazing ocean of possibility I see my Vortex as (I know - yuck, right? But that's how gross the idea is to me!) I'm sure you can come up with an equivalent metaphor for your own Vortex.

In fact, one of the things I ask my clients as they're designing their dream lives is, "Who do you want as your passenger when you're driving down your dream highway?"

I encourage them to think hard about this, because it's not enough just to have any old sisterhood. You need to have the RIGHT sisterhood with the right women, who are all heading in the same direction as you are. If you want to drink kombucha and your passengers all want to drink Coke, then beauty, it's going to be a miserable journey. Ditto if you want to listen to upbeat, funky tunes as you drive and they want 'Woe is me, everything sucks and the world is doomed!' emo crap.

You want to have people around you who love you enough to get excited for you when you're creating amazing stuff. And, by the same token, you want them to call you on your bullshit. You want them to hold you to the highest version of yourself. If you tell them that you're really struggling with something, you want them to say, "Well, duh: your language has been super-crappy lately - of course you're getting crappy results. How can you talk about this more intentionally and powerfully?"

So I'm going to invite you to take a look around you right now before you do anything else in this book. Who do you have in your life today who'll honor your new, 100% intentional Vortex, instead of making you feel weird about it?

And if your honest-to-God answer is, "Nobody!", then get yourself over to my free Facebook group, Ignite Your Queen Attract Your Soulmate at *www.facebook.com/groups/IgniteYourQueen*. Connect with the gorgeous sisterhood there: you'll find a network of thousands of beautiful, supportive women just waiting to encourage you in creating your dreams.

And in just the same way that you won't let anyone else 'shit in your Vortex', don't shit in there yourself either. The creations in your Vortex thrive on imagination, excitement, gratitude and positive expectation. They suffocate when you fill your Vortex with blaming, complaining, hiding from responsibility and fear. And it doesn't matter whether you're the one doing the imagining or the blaming, or whether it's someone else you listen to.

Either way, it has just as much impact. And either way, you need to be just as selective.

THE GOLD NUGGETS

Beautiful woman, we've covered some gold together in the last few pages. Here's a quick recap of the 24-Karat nuggets to take away with you and treasure as you head into the next chapter:

• 'Your Vortex' is the term I use for the limitless field of creative possibilities that you live within.

• You can visualize your Vortex in any way you want, as long as the visualization feels powerful to you.

• You'll attract whatever you fill your Vortex with into your external reality, so you need to be vigilant about the people (and thoughts) you allow into it.

GIFT WORK

Over to you, superstar! It's time for you to connect to your own EPIC Vortex.

Have you ever had the experience of using your Vortex to attract what you want? If so, I want you to close your eyes, put your hands on your heart, and connect to the memory of when it happened. This is a reference point for you. It's proof that you ARE an infinitely powerful creator / manifestor.

Connect back with the special ingredients that brought this thing into your life, so you KNOW you can do it again. Then ask yourself:

- What have you attracted into your life with ease?
- How did you feel about this desire before you called it in?
- Did you believe in it fully?
- Were you excited about it?

If you haven't yet connected to your Vortex, or you can't remember a time when you created from your Vortex, that's OK. I've got you, sister. It's time to get intimate with your Vortex right now. Here's how:

- Close your eyes and put your hands on your heart.
- Drop into your heart and really feel whatever you're feeling in there.
- Let your imagination take over and visualize your Vortex however it shows up for you.

CHAPTER TWO

Don't Treat This as Just Another
SELF-HELP BOOK

"Coaching without commitment is worthless. No true value or transformation will ever happen without full-blown commitment."

Before we go any deeper, beauty, we need to have a serious talk about self-help.

You see, I know how tempting it is to read book after book and join group after group, chasing the thing that will 'fix' you. But that just comes from lack. And trust me: you need to let that shit go.

You can't think - or read - your way to transformation. You have to feel whatever's there to deal with and move on from it - even if you can't feel anything at all right now.

That all starts with not adding anything more to your bookshelf... and instead, knowing that the goldmine is already inside of you, right now.

I DIDN'T WRITE THIS AS 'JUST ANOTHER SELF-HELP BOOK'

If you're anything like me, you've read approximately 7,351 self-help books over the course of your life. You've probably got a pile of them on your shelves at the moment. Some, no doubt, seemed pretty meh. Meanwhile, others had brilliant gems in them that made you see the whole world differently... at least while you were reading them, anyway. But I'll bet you almost anything that none of them truly transformed your life into the one you've dreamed of living. How do I know that? Because

- and I'm just gonna drop a truthbomb right here - you're reading THIS book now, looking for answers in it.

So it's a pretty safe bet that you haven't integrated what you've read.

The thing is, divine woman, that this ISN'T just another self-help book like the ones you've read before. It's going to demand a hell of a lot more from you for a start.

But, if you do the work within these chapters, and take the actions I recommend, I guarantee that it will guide you home to being the epic woman you were born to be. It will connect you with your inner Queen, who's more than capable of creating your life just the way you want it. No dream is too big for her. She has certainty, a killer mindset and a rock-solid belief system that anything she freaking desires is possible.

Reading this book and *doing the gift work* will amplify this version of you. It will give you permission to step into your Queen identity, which is who you actually are. You've held off stepping into that identity - held off putting on your crown - because you've been afraid that it won't last.

Well, superstar, it's time to trash that shithouse belief. It's been keeping you really, really small - so you need to step the fuck up. You're WAY too good to sell out on love (and on yourself) just because you haven't been able to make it work for you in the past. You're an incredible woman, and I need you to start embodying that.

Let's face it: the market is absolutely saturated with self-help books. When I type the term 'self-help' into Amazon's search bar, I get over 100,000 results. There's SO MUCH self-help content out there... but most women aren't any closer to living their dream lives than they were before they started reading.
So in this chapter, I want to explore why that is and talk a bit about how this book is different.

THE PARADOX OF THE PAST

There's a paradox you need to unravel when you start using your Vortex to call in your soulmate (or anything else your heart desires, for that matter). It's that, on the one hand, your past is irrelevant. It's gone. Happened. Finished with - namaste. But you also need to deal with it. You need to bring it to the surface, feel it and then heal it, so you CAN move on.

It doesn't matter what you've been able to do, have or create in the past. All that matters is creating your future - and you can get going with that right here, *right now,* wherever you're starting from.

So all those books that spend chapter after chapter delving into the reasons that you are the way you are? They might make you feel a little more self-aware, but they're NOT getting you any closer to your soulmate. They're definitely not getting you any closer to yourself.

With every one of them you read, trying to 'understand yourself better', you're just hiding behind not being ready. You're collecting more information, instead of committing to the deep work. Trust me: your soulmate is flat-out doing laps around your Vortex, waiting for you to be ready - and he's bloody exhausted.
So let's get cracking, shall we?

We all have crap from our pasts that we need to deal with. Your life is the way it is in the present because of past choices you've made. And yes, any time you chose not to choose, you still chose! That means you're 100% responsible for wherever you find yourself today. And if you don't like wherever that is? You need to figure out what your choices were, and start choosing differently.

I'll talk more about your life up till now later in the chapter. For the moment though, trust me that if you're a human being, you've experienced shit that you need to let go of. You can pretend to yourself that you don't, but you can't fool your Vortex. Whatever energy you're putting out, that's what you'll be getting back. And unless you deal with that shit (by, like I said above, feeling it, clearing it and letting it go), it's going to hang around.

It's going to pollute your Vortex and block you from creating what you want.

Let me be real with you here: dealing with past crap isn't comfortable. Not at all. There will be times in this book where you look at what I'm asking you to do and say, "Nope. Nuh-uh. I don't need to do that!"

But beauty, if you dig down into that refusal, I guarantee you'll find that underneath your, "I don't need to do that!" is a loud, blaring, "I don't WANT to do that." And I totally get that. On the other hand, I also know (through way, way too much life experience) that all those affirmations, gratitudes and positive thinking in other books aren't enough.

You can't just slap them on top of your internal shit heap and hope they'll work.

So what's the answer? You need to take responsibility NOW, from this moment forward, for everything you put into your Vortex. That involves accepting anything from your past that comes up and letting it come to the surface so you can transmute it into gold.

More than that, you need to stop blaming. No matter how tempting blame is, it robs you of your divine power. *Taking full responsibility* is the fastest way to take your power back so you can thrive in your life instead of feeling hopeless and stuck.

True transformation demands taking full responsibility for your shit before you can clear it out. Otherwise, it just doesn't work.

IF YOU NEED A PERMISSION SLIP, HERE IT IS

Another thing so many women in my programs tell me is that they love the idea of doing the work they discover in self-help books. But they never feel like they're allowed to do it.

They feel like their personal experiences are too small and insignificant to need healing. Or they believe their dreams are too selfish, too entitled, too airy-fairy, too high-maintenance, too 'not how their family rolls'... too whatever. Others think they're too much of a daydreamer, or not outgoing enough, or blah blah blah... the reasons are endless.

Almost without exception though, underneath the specifics, they believe they don't DESERVE the things they dream of.

So regardless of their why's, they can't bring themselves to commit 100% to creating their dream. They apologize for it on some level.

If this description is speaking to your soul, I totally understand. It took me almost 30 years to truly give myself permission to be all of who I am - to allow myself to want everything I wanted. I spent most of those 30 years apologizing for who I was. I thought I was too much, too big a personality, too spiritual, too intense, too deep and too sensitive.

No wonder I couldn't attract my soulmate. I was hangin' out in Shitsville where the zip code was woe is me!

The beginning of transformation for me was the moment I finally said, "No! Enough is enough! This stops now. This is who I fucking am, and I give myself permission to be ALL of her from now on. People who like me will love me, and people who don't weren't my people in the first place."

That was part of the sacred vow I mentioned in the last chapter - to never be anyone else other than who I truly was. And I knew right then that I was prepared to do WHATEVER it took to be that version of myself for the next 30, 40, 50 years... and the rest of my life.

I discovered that I'd never gotten over losing my dad at age eight. I realized I hadn't properly grieved him, and that I had some serious tears to release. I knew that if that meant crying for two days - or two weeks - solid, then I needed to give myself permission to do it. And once I let those healing tears flow whenever they needed to (which, by the way, was daily for two weeks), it felt *so good.*

Yes, it felt foreign and weird, because it was delayed grief... but it also felt incredibly cathartic. It brought me so much peace and alignment with my soul. I felt a massive shift in my heart space, and I refused to apologize for or justify it.

But the amazing thing was that when I opened myself to my grief, I also discovered other deep desires. I found a longing to go and put my heart and soul into acting - and I also found that I'd been swallowing a load of reasons about why I shouldn't, and how it was too late.

And now that I had my new permission slip, I decided that acting was exactly what I was going to do.

This permission helped me to follow through on other desires that I'd been stifling for years too. It helped me to uncover desires I'd totally forgotten I even had, because I'd been living life on autopilot. I got clear on exactly who I was - very sensitive, very emotional, very passionate, funny, deep, a little fiery, ALL these things.

And I committed to loving myself as I was, and unapologetically walking my path in its truest form.

PERMISSION TO HAVE WHAT YOU
WANT IS INCREDIBLY POWERFUL

The desire to have a family is something that SO MANY of my clients struggle with. I remember one woman in particular, Kristen, who swore that she didn't want children.

Kristen figured that kids wouldn't fit in with her high-powered, corporate lifestyle, so she'd never seriously thought about having them... or so she said, initially. The thing was that she was incredibly clever – she'd gone to university and got multiple degrees – but she'd never learned how to connect with her heart.

Once we started to uncover Kristen's shadow side though, it exposed a very different truth. Deep down, she realized that she believed she was 'damaged goods'. And she was terrified of inflicting that truth of herself onto her children.

Interestingly, the more she explored – and questioned – that belief, the more she was blown away by the strength of her longing to become a mother.

I remember the huge grin on Kristen's face when she finally gave herself permission to say, "I'm going to be a mother, and I'm going to have an amazing family." It was such a revelation for her, and once she really understood the work, she told me, "Oh my God, I've got my wings! I can fly and do whatever the hell I want!"

So if you need permission to be who you are and dream of what you're dreaming of, I invite you to give it to yourself, right now. If you can't quite manage that, go to the book bonuses page at *www.soultosoulglobal.com/book-bonuses* and download yourself a permission slip from me. Then fill it out, sign it and KNOW that you can do whatever the hell you desire.

YOU CAN'T *THINK* YOUR WAY INTO TRANSFORMATION

Look, I don't want to put down any specific self-help books here. There's truth in all of them, and everyone gets something different out of what they read. But the thing that 99.9% of the books I've read lack is a list of tangible steps to put into action.

Let's look at *The Secret*, for example. It was a fantastic book, and I loved it so much that I read it something like 456 times. BUT... it was also missing about ten chapters around how to connect with my shadow self and all the parts of me I was trying to hide. Without doing all of that *work*, none of the seeds of the book's ideas could take root in my mind and grow.

More than that, I was terrified to not be positive because of the way *The Secret* taught the Law of Attraction. I thought that accepting and feeling my shadow would attract terrible things to me. So instead, I did whatever I could to 'be positive'. I turned a blind eye to how I truly felt, deep down.

But all that hard-core positivity didn't manifest or attract what I wanted in love or in my bank account. Instead, it just left me disheartened, frustrated and feeling like trying to 'be positive' was a self-defeating spiral of failure.

In other words, it ended up making me feel even worse.

HOW NOT TO DO SELF-HELP

When I was trying to attract my soulmate, I did A LOT of intellectual self-help. I wrote affirmations – sometimes 22 times in a row for 30 days, because apparently, those were the magic numbers. I wrote down all the things I was grateful for in my gratitude journals. I put together vision boards of my perfect guy and perfect life. I took courses. I went to healers, kinesiologists and even psychics. You name it, I was doing it.

And, of course, I read self-help book after self-help book after self-help book. I absorbed a lot of information, but there was zero integration.

The problem was that I wasn't feeling excitement as I wrote my affirmations. I wasn't feeling any appreciation as I wrote my 'gratefuls' list. I couldn't feel any of that stuff because I was so disconnected from myself and my heart. I was avoiding dealing with everything deep down inside me that desperately needed to be expressed and felt.

It was almost like the affirmations and the positive thinking were icing I was putting on a cake that had a pile of rocks in it. I'd stand back and say, "Look at this beautiful, delicious cake I've baked!" Meanwhile, it was full of rocks that I was chipping my teeth on.

This kind of self-help was incredibly lazy because it was super-topline. I was just doing the bare minimum. I wasn't facing my truth, my shadow or my darkness. I didn't change my relationship with myself. I just tried to make transformation pretty... and darling woman, if there's one thing you know I don't recommend, it's putting a pretty bow around transformation.

I kept trying this kind of 'transformation' to call in my soulmate for eight fucking years. And all I attracted were drop-kicks who mirrored back to me how disconnected I was from myself.

The moment I changed the way I did self-help – and instead got 'down and dirty' with who I really was – my soulmate stopped doing laps around me. It was literally only three months after that until I met my epic hubs, the love of my life, Anaam.

I just wish I'd started sooner (but I also believe in divine timing, and that I was meant to go on that journey for my soul).

The good news is that you don't have to spend EIGHT YEARS to attract your soulmate. (Of course, if you've already spent this long, it's OK. It's all part of your journey.) *Soul to Soul,* my signature program to get women into their hearts, moves you into alignment in just eight weeks. But to see results like that, you have to get over the idea of transformation as something that happens in your head, or something that happens TO you. Instead, you have to roll up your sleeves, commit like it's life or death, and play full-out.

That's because transformation is something that takes place in your heart and your soul. That's why I called my program Soul to Soul (although all my rockstar clients call it a homecoming!)

And I promise you that until you accept and work with your heart fully, transformation won't happen for you - and nothing will change.

YES, YOU HAVE CHILDHOOD STUFF

I can generally divide my clients into two groups:

- Women in the first group drop right down into their shadow selves straight away. They say something like, "Oh my gosh, I knew I needed to do the work, but I didn't realize how deep I'd need to go.

I thought it was just a tweak. I didn't realize how disconnected I was from myself and my dreams."

- Women in the second group push back and say something like, "I don't need to do this stuff. I had a great childhood with no issues. Can I get on with attracting my perfect soulmate now, please?"

The women in the second group tend to be the ones who come to me with 'jazz hands energy'. They insist, with brilliant smiles and - sometimes literal - jazz hands, that they're totally fine as they are. They talk about their great job, their great life and all the great places they travel to. And they think that whatever's wrong with their lives is about a guy, their weight or where they live.

But the women who are hungry to do the work soon realize that they were totally disconnected from what they wanted. They discover that their smile was a façade - a 'happy face' mask they'd been wearing as their public persona - and it wasn't working.

What these women didn't know at the beginning was that it doesn't matter how wonderful your childhood was. It doesn't matter if your dad packed your school lunch for you every single day. It doesn't matter if your mum picked you up from school at 3pm on the dot. It doesn't matter if your parents had the strongest marriage on the face of the planet. Don't get me wrong: it's beautiful if all of that's true for you. But it still doesn't mean that your inner little girl (more about her in Chapter 7) got what she needed emotionally from them.

What matters is that if you're not where you want to be today, I guarantee the roots of that situation lie somewhere in your childhood.

For example, if you're still single at 31 (or at 40+) and you don't want to be, then SOMETHING that your little girl experienced created that situation. It might not be something huge and traumatic. It might be something that your adult self thinks you just need to 'get over' and forget about. But until you deal with your little girl's reactions to it, you're delaying getting what you really want.

Sometimes, the roots might lie in having grown up in a 'lack' household. Maybe your little girl always got just enough of everything to meet her needs, but never anything more. Or maybe she always got the material stuff she needed, but never got the love, approval, recognition or support that she craved emotionally.

Whatever it was, this isn't about blaming your parents. As a mum myself, I believe that - with maybe a few dramatic exceptions - parents do the absolute best they can with what they know.

But, as a result of how you grew up, chances are very high that you've picked up some core beliefs that don't serve you about yourself and the world. So if you're tempted to sit back and be one of those women above who 'had a great childhood', I invite you to reconsider.

If you want love to work for you,
you need to do the work yourself.

Remind yourself that we all have shit to clean up. That's not about making yourself wrong or getting bogged down by all the shit. It's simply about acknowledging that the shit is there, and that it needs to be released.

Then, as soon as you start to release it, magic will happen. You'll start to attract the things you want the moment you refuse to tolerate not having them for one more minute.

LET THIS BE THE LAST SELF-HELP BOOK YOU BUY FOR A LONG TIME

I said at the beginning of this chapter that I didn't write this as 'just another self-help book'. But the truth is that YOU'RE the one who determines whether that's what it ends up being or not.

If you treat what you're reading as 'just another self-help book', then that's all it will be. If you simply read it, take away an AHA moment or two, then put it on your bookshelf and move on to the next one, it'll never be anything else.

If, on the other hand, you treat this book as the gift it is, it can be so much more for you.

So I invite you to read it over and over again until the pages are well-loved and a little ragged. Make notes in the margins. Go away and do the activities (the gift work at the end of each chapter), and make more notes about what you did and any results. Milk the content in here for all it's worth.

If you do all of that, this book will be your key to a kingdom where you can create whatever the fuck you want in your life. It will be the vehicle that brings you not just the man you're longing for, but also your dream business, and anything else your heart desires.

And YOU'RE the one who gets to make that call. Something I say to my Soul to Soul clients when they enroll is, "From this moment on, you need to CHOOSE that this will be the process that changes your life. No hoping or trying. Just full-blown commitment and declaring that this is it."

When they do that, they're astounded that the results they get far exceed their already high expectations. And it's all because they set an intention that they packed with power and certainty.

I know that it sounds daunting to dig down deep into your stuff. But sister, if you don't, you'll cut yourself off from being able to create the life you really desire. So stay with me, because in the next chapter we'll talk about the pain that comes up when you start digging - and what to do with it once you uncover it.

THE GOLD NUGGETS

Beautiful woman, we've covered some gold together in the last few pages. Here's a quick recap of the 24-karat nuggets to take away with you and treasure as you head into the next chapter:

- If you're like most of the women I work with, you probably already have a library of self-help books sitting on your shelf.

- No matter how many of them you read though, they never work - because you keep looking for easy answers when there's deep work to do.

- That deep work starts with looking at all the 'stuff' from your childhood that you've pushed down where you don't have to face it (and yes, you DO have that stuff).

- If you commit to doing this work with your full passion and heart, you'll see your world start to transform as if by magic.

GIFT WORK

Over to you, superstar! This is your moment of truth, the moment where you get to commit to playing full-out with the information in this book. Let's do this!

If you haven't already, download your permission slip from my website (go to *www.soultosoulglobal.com/book-bonuses*), print it out and fill it in. Put it somewhere you'll see it every day: perhaps your bathroom mirror or up next to your bed. Remind yourself that you have permission to do whatever the fuck you want!

Take out your journal - or get one if you don't already have one - because you'll be needing it! Write out how it feels to fully commit to the processes in this book.

Connect back with the special ingredients that brought this thing into your life, so you KNOW you can do it again. Then ask yourself:

- What scares you?
- What feels daunting?
- Do you have a glimmer of excitement under all that fear that you can catch hold of and expand?
- How do you want to feel in your skin and in your life?
- Where do you want to be one year from now?
- How do you want to feel in a divine, soul-connected relationship?

Write it all down, darling woman, and get ready to roll with your desires!

CHAPTER THREE

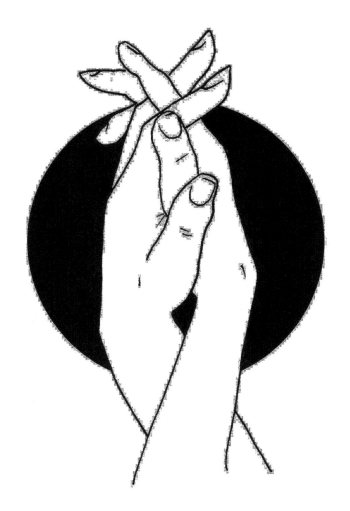

You DON'T Have
TO SUFFER

"When you feel grateful for your obstacles, you're on the fast track to your dreams."

In Chapter 2, I told you that you need to face your pain and experience it before you can let it go - and that's 100% true. You need to connect with and acknowledge your pain... and more importantly, you need to feel it.

But what you DON'T have to do is allow your pain to make you suffer. Does that sound like a contradiction in terms, darling one? If so, buckle up. Because this chapter - where you'll learn the difference between pain and suffering, and how to choose one over the other - will blow your mind.

THERE'S A DIFFERENCE BETWEEN 'PAIN' AND 'SUFFERING'

Let me start by saying that this isn't a book where I try to tell you that everything in life is unicorns and rainbows. The bottom line is that we ALL experience pain in this lifetime. It might be physical pain. It might be emotional pain. It might even be spiritual pain. Regardless: we're human beings, so pain is unavoidable.

BUT... pain is the intense hurt and discomfort that happens in the moment. It's the flash of agony as you twist your ankle, or the heartbreak as you say goodbye to someone you love. Suffering, on the other hand, is your response to that original pain. It's the fear and resistance (and sometimes guilt or shame) you develop based on what you make the original pain mean.
Suffering can go on for months, years or even decades after the

original pain - but it doesn't have to.

Suffering is also highly addictive - it's a tempting way to avoid taking responsibility for your own life. You can make suffering mean that you're a virtuous person or that you've had it tough. You can also make it mean that you couldn't possibly do anything differently to how you've done it so far. That then lets you off the hook from having to actually deal with your pain and transmute it.

Your lower self feeds off this suffering and wants you to stay there - partly because we humans know how to do suffering well. Plus, all that suffering is also a way to get attention (although from the wrong place!) Meanwhile, your higher self - that part I've been calling 'your Queen' - knows you'll never achieve anything powerful if you just *accept* your suffering. She wants to transmute the shit out of your pain and turn it into gold and new opportunities.

Whether or not you lift yourself out of this rut comes down to one thing: a decision. You can either decide, *"Yes, I want to keep feeling my pain and using it as an excuse to hold myself back from getting what I want."* OR you can decide, *"NO! Fuck that! I'm done. Enough is enough. I'm ready to feel it and heal it, so I can create my life the way I want it!"*

The key thing I want you to understand is that it's always 100% up to us how we respond to pain. I've seen different people respond to exactly the same painful situation in different ways.

And how they respond always, always, ALWAYS determines what happens next in their lives.

I'm not just talking about the little things in life there either. I've seen different people respond differently to something as huge as a cancer diagnosis. I've seen one person say, "Oh my God, my life is over, and I need to start preparing to die now!" Meanwhile, another will say, "OK, this happened. What could be good about it? How can I deepen and grow?"... and then genuinely look for an answer that serves them.

I've seen the same choices - and yes, beautiful woman, it IS a choice - play out in stories of shitty childhoods with alcoholic parents, sexual abuse, illness and more. One person says, "This happened to me, and now it's all I can ever be."

They choose suffering by making their pain the defining feature of their life. Meanwhile, another says, "This happened, and it sucked… but it doesn't define me. I can choose a different story going forward, and my abuse is not who I am."

That second person acknowledges their pain, but doesn't descend into suffering.

YOU ALWAYS HAVE A CHOICE ABOUT HOW YOU RESPOND

Melanie, a lovely woman who did my program, had so much repressed anger when she came to me.

She'd had an extremely tough childhood with super-strict, controlling parents who gave her no voice in her relationships or her life. Then she went on to develop an autoimmune disease, which she felt was incredibly unfair.

Melanie was addicted to the suffering her condition created, so of course she didn't like me saying that suffering is a choice. But I'm a straight shooter, so I told her, "Until you're willing to admit to yourself that this is a choice — until you're willing to give up the victimhood / blame paradigm that's eating you alive — I can't help you. Nobody can."

Understandably, hearing this hit Melanie like a ton of bricks. I was speaking directly to her way of being, and her inner little girl didn't like this one bit. She'd been very happy holding Melanie back from her greatness, and now I was calling her out on it.

Melanie chose to step up, recognizing that this suffering / blame energy was spread all through her life. She took responsibility for addressing it, took her life back, and hasn't looked back since.

Now if you're reading this idea for the first time, it might sound pretty freaking confronting. You might find yourself thinking, *"But Lucy, you don't understand! My history is different! I can't just get over it that easily. I can't pretend it never existed!"*

If that's you, I want you to know that I'm not telling you to pretend it never existed. Far from it! I'll talk about this more later in the chapter, but for now, please understand that I'm not telling you to 'pretend'.

You get to respond to your pain however you like. Just be aware that the response you choose determines what you'll experience in the future. In Chapter 4, we'll talk a bit more about exactly how to choose your response. But before we get to that, I want you to get super-clear on the concept that no matter what happens to you, you get to choose what you'll make it mean. You get to choose how it affects your life going forward.

Or, in the words of the ancient Buddhist saying, **"Pain is inevitable, but suffering is optional."**

Understanding this is at the core of taking your own power back.

YOU HAVE A CHOICE IN EVERY MOMENT OF EVERY SINGLE DAY

I've worked with so many clients who were attached to their suffering. And I get it - truly. When you've been through something traumatic, been diagnosed with a serious illness or had massive heartbreak, it can feel like...

- You've EARNED the right to feel shitty about it.
- You've EARNED the right to wallow, feel sorry for yourself and develop a load of negative beliefs.
- You've EARNED the right to see yourself as a powerless victim and just stop trying (because you know you'll never have what you want anyway).

And you know what? I'm not telling you that you haven't earned that right. But what I am saying is that wallowing in the experience is keeping you stuck in the past, in suffering and in a big, fat holding pattern. It's stopping you from having the lit-up life that you deserve in the present. The life I'm pretty sure you want deep down.

OK, it's time for another truthbomb, divine woman - I'm not here to waste your time by keeping it all cutesy. Every action has an outcome. Every choice has a consequence. So if you DO choose to spend time hanging out in Victim Village, you can't expect to get what you truly want in life. You can't expect to attract that high-vibrational soulmate, or that full bank account from living a life on purpose you dream of, or anything from your highest vibration, for that matter. Why? Because victimhood breeds empty dreams.

So until you accept that YOU'RE the only one with the power to choose your response to whatever happens to you, you'll never actually step into that power.

I know it's not easy or comfortable to hear, but nothing truly important ever is.

You can choose to hang onto your old story and keep suffering and playing small. But the fact that you're reading this book tells me you're well and truly done with not getting what you want. You're ready to try something different.

And whether you choose to rise or stay where you are, it IS a choice - and it's one that will determine the future you live into. You're making those kinds of choices over and over again in every moment, and living consciously means making them intentionally.

So right now, I want you to close your eyes and put your hand on your heart. Scan back over the past year. What choices do you notice yourself consistently making that have kept you in the same outcome in your life?

What might it be like to choose differently?

ASK YOURSELF HOW YOUR CHOICES FEEL IN THE MOMENT

Many of the women who work with me arrive with stories and belief systems that are either based on their own experiences, or that they've inherited from their parents. These might be:

- Relationship stories like, 'All the good men are taken. You can't trust men. They cheat or only end up leaving you anyway.'
- Money stories like, 'Our family doesn't need a lot of money - we're good at making do.'
- Career stories like, 'Of course you'll be a nurse! That's what all the women in our family do.'

And whether the stories you tell yourself come from your own past or someone else's, there's a foolproof way to figure out whether they're serving you or not:

Just ask yourself how each choice makes you feel.

Start by identifying the story or choice that's clearest and most present in your mind, and ask your heart, *"Does this feel good? Will it help me to create the kind of life I want?"*

Then close your eyes, put your hands over your heart and connect with the answer.
This might feel challenging - after all, it's not something we're taught

to do in today's world. So give yourself a little time and space to allow the answer to come up. If it's 'Yes', that's great. If not, ask yourself what choice would make you feel better (and again, we'll dive deeper into this in Chapter 4).

Once you've found your answer for one question, move on to the next. Give yourself permission to question everything.

Your life is made up of choices. When you add all those choices up, what you get is the life you're currently living.

So make sure all your choices are supportive ones that move you closer to the life you want to live right now!

THIS DOESN'T HAVE TO BE COMPLICATED

While I'm the first to acknowledge that stepping into your power to choose can feel super-uncomfortable, what it shouldn't be is complicated.

In fact, I guarantee that if anything feels complicated, it's a sign you're resisting something that - somewhere deep inside yourself - you already know. It's a sign that you're falling back into automatic thinking.

The truth is that it's simple. Not always easy, sure, but simple. To the point where this chapter is possibly the most 'back-to-basics' one in the book.

So if you find yourself feeling like something's hugely complicated, I want you to take a step back and ask yourself one simple question: *"What the fuck am I choosing right now?"*

That might sound harsh, but it works like a pattern interrupt to break your train of habitual, automatic thinking. It allows you to question yourself and your thoughts - something you need to do every single day if you want to move beyond the subtle, subconscious messages of powerlessness you've taken on board throughout your life.

EVERYTHING YOU DO IS A CHOICE

If you leave this chapter with just one message, I want it to be this: EVERYTHING you think, do or say in your life is a choice. I'm not saying you control everything you experience. Like I said at the beginning of this chapter, shit happens. Pain is real. Of *course* it's real.

But you get to choose how you'll respond to that pain - just like you can choose how you respond to anything else in your life. In fact, every time you respond to anything, it's a choice. Again, like I said earlier, even choosing NOT to choose is a choice.
In fact, you might not want to hear this, but you're making a choice in how you're receiving the information in this chapter as you read it. Maybe you choose to hear it as something exciting and liberating - something that FINALLY puts you in the driver's seat of your life. Or maybe, instead, you choose to hear it as a message of blame - one that means I'm telling you that wherever you are in this moment is your own fault. (Because you believe it has to be *somebody's* fault, and if you can't blame other people, the only person you can blame is yourself.)

And again, I get this. I've had so many women come to me attached to their struggles and committed to the idea that they have to suffer. They insist that:

- Things just don't work out for them.
- This is just their lot in life.
- They're just not good at relationships (or money, or achieving their goals, or... or... or).

But you know what? Once they start working with me, most of them very quickly realize that they DO have a choice. They choose to grab their life with both hands, and literally change it from one day to the next.

Yep, life can absolutely transform that fast. One of the golden nuggets I want you to take away from this is that change can happen extremely quickly. You just need to be ready to step up and do what it takes to make yourself the priority. And beauty, that means being prepared and willing to dig deep.

So many of my clients have AHA moments where they recognize that they CAN take responsibility for the way they respond to whatever they experience. When they realize that, they feel liberated. And suddenly, the Universe tilts on its axis. Life magically starts going their way. They realize that they can think and speak whatever they want into existence - and it works.
BUT... there are always a few who don't let that acknowledgment of choice land. Accepting it would completely betray everything they believe about themselves. And so, instead, they choose to go on suffering.

Again, that's fine - I'm all about free choice. But you wouldn't believe how many of them come back to me a year or two later, saying, "Lucy, I'm so angry with myself. I chose my suffering and fear instead of my dream, and nothing has changed."
And all I can say is, "Yep. You sure did. So - what are you going to choose now?"

Here's the thing: until it's about you, it's never going to be about you.

Actually take that in. This is a big one for my clients. They tell me, "But Lucy, this person really needs me right now!" There's always someone or something else they prioritize. Until they stop it, they keep coming last in their lives, because they keep putting everyone else first.

Again, however you choose to let the information in this book land and respond to it, it's OK. You can get excited about climbing into the driver's seat of your life and putting your Queen behind the steering wheel. Or you can refuse to acknowledge that it's possible, and instead let your little girl (who can barely even see over the dashboard) lead the way.

But darling woman, if you choose the latter, there's ZERO point in reading any further. Choosing to take responsibility is a vital part of changing your life. Your response has to be, "Hellz, yes! I'm willing to choose something way better for myself!"

Otherwise, you can just expect a shitload more Groundhog Day, and I'm SO not an advocate for that.

Just ask yourself that question from earlier: which option do you think will get you closer to your dream and living your life the way you want it?

THIS WAS SO CLEAR AFTER MY FIRST MISCARRIAGE

Back in 2017, I was two months pregnant with my first baby. One morning, I had what I thought would be a totally routine hospital check-up the same day as I was co-hosting and speaking at a big event.

I went to my check-up, and I can still remember my shock and devastation when the sonographer told me she couldn't hear a heartbeat. It was like a punch straight through my gut. Right in that moment, all I felt was utter disbelief and heartbreak. Like I said, I'd never claim that pain doesn't exist or that it's not real. That moment hurt like hell, and I cried all the way home until right before the event.

At the same time, I knew this experience could be – if I allowed it to – a huge gift to me. It could be a way for the Universe to tap me on the shoulder and guide me to deepen even more than I'd been able to before. It could elevate me and move me forward... or it could eat me alive.

And the only person who could choose which one it would be was me.

So when I got back to the car, after the first wave of grief had passed,

I realized that I had a choice ahead of me. I could cancel the event, go home, go to bed and cry many more tears, and I doubt anyone would have blamed me. OR I could commit to showing up as my authentic self and tell the room what had happened.

I gave myself the space to feel into the choice. And I realized I felt strongly in my heart that the more powerful option for me was to show up, without any idea of how it would go. It wasn't about pushing through my grief and refusing to acknowledge it. It wasn't about proving anything or standing in a place of 'look how strong and committed I am to my work!' And it definitely wasn't about doing 'jazz hands' and pretending everything was fine when it wasn't.

Instead, it was about acknowledging an opportunity to be present at the event in my raw vulnerability, my fragility and my authenticity. It was a new space for me to step into, and it felt right.

So I trusted my instincts, and I went to the event.

I didn't try to work it all out in advance. I just started the event by saying, "Hey, guys – I found out I had a miscarriage earlier today. I'm really hurting and still in shock. But I still wanted to be here tonight to give you an opportunity to see me when I haven't got everything together. I think these moments open up space to connect on a deeper level."

I told everyone there that I wouldn't edit myself. I'd let myself cry if I needed to. And if I couldn't stop, I'd just remove myself from the floor, so they could keep going without me. I told them, "I just want you to know that this could happen. I don't know if it will, but it could – and I'm OK with that."

That level of truth, of simply being who I was without figuring everything out in advance, deeply resonated with a lot of the women there. Sure, a few of them found it inconvenient that the event topic had shifted so dramatically. But most of them were on the edge of their seats, hanging off every word and thanking me afterward for sharing myself so generously and openly.

There was even one woman who'd just lost her mother and was in a very dark place. She connected so deeply with my vulnerability that she went on to become a client the next day.
It felt incredible to be able to reach the hearts of women who needed that level of truth, and I'll never forget it.

IT'S NOT ABOUT PUSHING THINGS DOWN (OR AWAY, OR AT ALL)

I want you to know that I'm not telling you the story of my miscarriage to put pressure on you. Everyone's totally different.

Perhaps, in the same situation, your most authentic, vulnerable response would have been to go home and give yourself the space and permission to grieve alone. And maybe, for you, speaking at the event would have meant pushing yourself to prove something. Maybe it would have meant you were trying to avoid the shock and grief, and that you were forcing yourself to pretend that nothing was wrong.

If so, then it would absolutely have been the most powerful option for you to choose to love on yourself, stay home and follow what your heart was telling you it needed.

We'll talk more in Chapter 8 about why pretending everything's fine doesn't work. In fact, giving yourself permission to feel all the shit you've refused to feel in the past - the shit you've been numbing yourself to avoid feeling - is an integral part of getting the life you want.

For now though, I want you to come back to the two core ideas of this chapter. Firstly, that whatever you do, say or think in response to what you experience is your choice. And secondly, when you have a choice between two (or more) options, pick the one that:

- Feels best in your heart and soul.
- Makes the boat go faster toward your dream.

This concept of our response to everything in life being a choice doesn't just hold true for huge, deeply emotional life situations like births, deaths, illnesses and breakups. It's also true for the relationship you have with money.

VALUING YOURSELF MEANS INVESTING IN YOURSELF

I see this all the time when women come to work with me. The money stories – their fears of scarcity and the program not working – inevitably come up. And one of my clients, Sarah, is a great example of this.

When Sarah first contacted me, she had an agreement with herself that she wouldn't sign up for my program (or any program) if it was more than $500. But then, when she jumped onto the call, our conversation ignited her soul and inspired her to take action.

However, she didn't want to admit that she was worth far more than $500, and that she deserved to invest in herself. Because *of that, she started sabotaging the call by not showing up fully until I called her on it. She knew she had powerhouse inside her, but she admitted that on most days, she only lived up to 10% of her potential.*

She also realized that she kept herself hidden from others, and even from herself. And perhaps most importantly, she acknowledged that if she didn't invest in herself now, she might never meet her soulmate and live her full potential.

So she chose to look at her pain, connect with it and feel it. But she also chose to no longer let it own her or keep her suffering.
After that choice, she hit the ground running. The minute she realized she was worth a LOT more than $500, something shifted deep within her. Once she acknowledged her 'deserve-ability', it suddenly illuminated her value from within.

Everything she'd buried deep within herself for so long surfaced for healing. She shared that she'd never, ever felt seen, held and supported for who she really was. She jokes about it now, but at the time, it was a revelation. The fact that she lived her life with so much pain and restriction without noticing that it bled across her entire life blew her mind. Not to mention the realization that she was always last on the priority list, but still kept playing the victim.

The happy ending to this story is that Sarah's currently up-leveled in every area of her life. She has changed careers, is now with her soulmate and is 100% living on purpose.

HOW WOULD YOU LIVE IF EVERYTHING WAS RIGGED IN YOUR FAVOR?

If you're still struggling with the idea that you can choose to respond however you want to whatever happens to you, I understand.

For the longest time, I told myself that losing my father when I was eight meant that I'd never allow myself to love again. I loved him so much, and then he was just... gone. And the story I told myself about it was that it wasn't safe to love anyone, ever again.

As I grew older, that story transformed. It mutated into, 'I'm not good at relationships', 'I'm just scared of committing to any one person' and 'I refuse to go through feeling abandoned again'. I allowed these new stories to keep me living in my victimhood - a place where I was powerless to do anything.

As far as I was concerned, it was all due to my father dying, and those were just the cards I'd been dealt.

My stories created walls between me and the soulmate and life that I longed for in my heart. And it took putting a completely different lens on what I'd experienced to break through them. I had to start asking myself a version of a question that dates all the way back to Rumi: *"What if everything that had happened - including my dad's death - was actually rigged in my favor?"* What would I choose, and how would I show up if that were true?

The truth is that I wouldn't be writing this book or doing the work I'm doing in the world if I hadn't experienced such deep trauma and grief. I'm grateful to my dad for putting me on this path. Don't get me wrong: I miss him like crazy. I'd do anything to have him back. But I'm also grateful for all the deep work I've chosen to do in first healing my own heart, and then helping so many women in the world to do the same.

So right now, I invite you to ask yourself the same question. What meaning are you assigning to all the things that haven't worked out the way you'd wished or intended that they would? Are you telling yourself that life has to be hard, and that this is just the way it is? If so, what new lens could you use to view your experiences, and what new choices could you make?

What could your life look like if you truly believed that everything was rigged in your favor?

THE GOLD NUGGETS

Beautiful woman, we've covered some gold together in the last few pages. Here's a quick recap of the 24-karat nuggets to take away with you and treasure as you head into the next chapter:

- You might think that the words 'pain' and 'suffering' are interchangeable, but there's a world of difference between the concepts.

- 'Pain' is the intense sensation you feel in the moment something hurts you, while 'suffering' is how you respond to and relive that pain over and over again afterward.

- You get to choose the way you respond to the pain in your life - and whether you suffer because of it.

- You make that choice through the meaning you give to each of the events in your life.

- You're always free to choose, no matter what. Ask, "What if life were rigged in my favor?" and, "How can I reframe digging up the weeds of my childhood stuff to make it fun, light and exciting?"

- That deep work starts with looking at all the 'stuff' from your childhood that you've pushed down where you don't have to face it (and yes, you DO have that stuff).

· If you commit to doing this work with your full passion and heart, you'll see your world start to transform as if by magic.

GIFT WORK

Over to you, superstar! It's time to take a look at your choices around your pain and how you choose to live now. Get into the juicy bits by doing the actions below.

First up, meditation time! I love a good guided meditation. Head to the book bonuses page on my website at:
www.soultosoulglobal.com/book-bonuses
to download and listen to a supercharged meditation that can clear a lot of dense energy. Find a nice, quiet place to tune in and let yourself deeply absorb it.

Now grab your journal, darling woman. It's time to get some clarity. Write down whatever stories have come up for you as you read this chapter, using the following questions as a guide:

· Where in your life are you defining yourself by your suffering, rather than acknowledging the pain and moving on?
· What CHOICES are you making about how your life looks?
· What story have you been clinging to that's been keeping you in shackles?

It's time to let go of those stories and write a brand-new one that lights up your soul. So make time to journal out your answers and really go deep.

There's gold to be found if you let yourself go there.

CHAPTER FOUR

The Power of The
REFRAME

"'I can't do it' will keep you exactly where you are. 'I can and I will' will change your life."

In Chapter 3, I told you that you could choose the meaning of anything that happens to you. And part of making this choice is choosing how you talk about your experience.

Why? Because believe me, sister: every single word you speak carries a vibration, and it impacts your life directly. Your words are literally MAGIC. They're spells - and if you cast them powerfully, they'll bring everything you dream of into your reality.

But you have to be deliberate and intentional with your language. If you're lazy and use shitty, low-vibrational words, you'll attract shitty, low-vibrational experiences - and I know you don't want to do that to yourself, divine woman.

So in this chapter, you'll learn how to see and speak about things differently, every single time.

REFRAMING CAN CHANGE YOUR LIFE

'Reframing' simply means taking an experience you've had and putting a different frame around it to see it differently. Reframing is designed to move you forward instead of sitting still, stuck in resistance.

What do I mean by that? Well, imagine a set of two picture frames. One's beautiful, elegant and super-classy. The other is cheap, scuffed and coming apart at one corner.

Now imagine you have an abstract painting that you want to hang on your wall. To hang it there, you need to first put it in a frame... and it's going to look completely different depending on the frame you choose. Put it in the beautiful frame, and it's going to look amazing on your wall. But put it in the cheap frame... and it'll look like something you picked up at the local dollar store.

It's exactly the same with the way you look back on the experiences you've been through in your life (or even the experiences you're having right NOW). I started to talk about this in the last chapter when I told you about my miscarriage.

I could have looked at it through the cheap, falling-apart frame of, 'Oh my God, this is the most devastating thing that could have ever happened! The loss and grief and pain are paralyzing! I can't cope and I'll never get over this!' Or I could search for a different frame to view it through, like the one I ended up choosing - one of, 'This is incredibly painful right now, but I also KNOW it's an opportunity for me to deepen into my heart and to show up even more authentically.'

Once you've chosen to believe that 'everything is rigged in your favor', it's just a matter of being willing to look for a frame for your experience that fits that belief. This is a completely new way to live your life. My clients can't get enough of reframing once they 'get it' - they feel it as a new power being unleashed inside of them.

Another way of looking at reframing is imagining it as a GPS that works 24/7 to help you navigate the inevitable bumps, detours and roadblocks of life. It's a tool that helps you to actually see - not just believe - that life doesn't have to be hard.

In fact, reframing shows you that the better it gets, the better it gets.

THE MANTRA THAT WILL STOP YOU FROM SUFFERING EVER AGAIN

Mastering the art of the reframe won't stop you from experiencing painful things in your life. We talked about this in Chapter 3: challenging, uncomfortable experiences are simply part of being human. They're inevitable.

What reframing will do is bring suffering to a grinding halt in your life - right now and forever. Remember that there's a big difference between pain and suffering. Suffering is a choice. I hope you can see that clearly now, because it was an absolute game-changer for me - as it has been for so many women I've mentored.

So how can you possibly reframe something that feels overwhelmingly painful in the moment? Well, the first thing is not to try - not in THAT moment, anyway. Remember: we're not going for 'push energy' here. We're not trying to shove the pain down or pretend it doesn't exist. So if there's pain there, let yourself feel it... like, really feel it. Cry or scream or do whatever you need to do in response, and let it rip, baby!

Get that shit out of your system, so you're not carrying it around with you.

Eventually though, there'll be a point where the tears stop. You'll realize you don't need to cry anymore - or at least, not right now. And then, once the dust has settled and you're feeling less affected, you'll have a choice about how you'll view the experience that caused you pain moving forward.

Once you get to that moment, I want you to ask yourself one simple question:

"What could be GOOD about this situation?"

Make this your new favorite mantra. No matter what happens, ask yourself what could be good about it. What gold could there be in this apparently shitty situation? That gold may not show itself right off the bat, but trust me - it's there. And looking at things this way is part of the brand-new mindset you're building. Once thinking in these terms becomes second nature, it will set you up for success in every area of your life.

When you ask yourself that question, you might find that a clear answer pops straight into your mind. If so, that's awesome - and the more often you do this practice, the more quickly an answer is likely to arrive.

But if you don't get an immediate answer, that's OK too. Keep coming back to the question and checking in with it. Each time, ask it with an open mind, genuine curiosity and a willingness to receive whatever answer might come up for you.

Regardless of the response you get though, I guarantee that just asking the question will start to lift you out of the suffering you're experiencing in that moment. It will help you to move beyond your automatic reactions, and beyond the chaos and the drama.

Then, once you get the hang of it, you'll get pretty addicted to a good reframe. You'll start feeling a lot of possibilities and an expansive energy opening up inside of you. I can already see you cracking a cheeky smile as you say to yourself, *"Yep, you know, this reframe stuff is pretty damn cool."*

FOR EPIC TRANSFORMATION, YOU ALSO NEED TO REFRAME YOUR IDENTITY

Say what now? OK, hear me out.

On the surface, it looks like one thing to reframe a specific experience. It seems like another altogether to reframe your entire identity.

But I want you to know, superstar, that reframing your identity is ABSOLUTELY possible to do. So many women - like thousands of them - come to me with shitty, victim-based identities. Sometimes they're consciously aware of it. Most often though, they have no idea. They have to dig deep to find the beliefs and stories that make up their overall identity.

When they do, they often find cheap, crappy frames like:

- 'The trauma / abuse / neglect / whatever I experienced means I'm damaged goods and no one will want me.'
- 'It's not safe to love anyone with my whole heart.' (You might remember that I had this one!)
- 'I'm never going to be as important to other people as they are to me.'
- 'Love never works out for me.'
- 'Men don't choose me.'

Personally, one of the most powerful identity reframes I've ever discovered - the one that creates the highest meaning for my painful experiences - is this:

'The further I've fallen, the higher I can rise.'

Other examples of reframes you could try might include:

- 'My experiences have given me a depth of compassion for people in this situation that I'd never have been able to access otherwise.'
- 'Not having my needs met as a child meant I grew up to be resourceful and learned how to do things for myself.'
- 'Never feeling important has given me a chance to learn how to put myself first and show other people how to treat me like the Queen that I am.'
- 'I used to attract men who didn't show up for me, but right now, I AM soulmate material. My perfect relationship exists because I exist. I'm learning what being in a soulmate relationship with myself feels like first so that I can attract it in. I know he's going to flow into my life when I least expect it, because I'll be so busy loving on me.'

Again, this isn't about pretending that your experiences didn't hurt like hell. We'll talk more in Chapter 7 about how your inner little girl pushed down all the pain, grief and confusion she felt when she didn't get the love and support she needed. And we'll talk more about why you've GOT to allow that to surface so you can feel it and heal it too.

In the meantime, understand that until you feel everything she pushed away, she'll keep sabotaging your life. She'll keep shitting in your Vortex, and you'll never truly be free of the crap. It doesn't matter how many reframes you try to do. You'll just continue to live that godawful Groundhog Day, and I know you're reading this book to put an end to that.

BUT... then, after you've felt all that pain and moved through it, you have a choice. You can choose how you'll view yourself as a person when you look back at the experience. That's when you'll have your chance to use your new favorite mantra: 'What could be good about this?'

And that's when you have the power to decide what you'll create in your Vortex. That's when you can up-level and recreate a powerful new identity that serves you. The trick is to embody and be a woman who's in a thriving relationship RIGHT NOW. How does she think? How does she show up for herself?

You need to be that woman now in order to step into her shoes and live the life you've always dreamed of.

IS YOUR IDENTITY
REALLY EVEN YOURS?

One of my clients, Jessica, was an accountant who – ironically – had a ton of debt. Even more ironically, this naturally beautiful woman had spent a LOT of money on plastic surgery because she thought her struggles in love were due to 'not being pretty enough'.

As we worked together, she realized that this came from having a distant, unaffectionate, emotionally unavailable father. Her inner little girl believed that if she was just 'prettier', her dad would see her and approve of her. So, she'd got the work done on her face to 'solve all her problems', not realizing that it just racked up a lot of debt and anxiety. Plus, it kept her looking externally for happiness.

On top of that, she was carrying stories of scarcity and not-enough-ness from her mother. Her huge AHA moment came when she fully understood that these weren't her stories. She realized that she could choose a new story for herself – one that honored who she was and where she was headed in life.

And she could do it on her terms.

Jessica had to reframe what she thought was her money issue and realize that it wasn't even hers. It belonged to her parents. Once she did that, things started to change – fast!

Now, Jessica is absolutely thriving. She's debt-free, she's changed careers and she's living on purpose. Not only that, but she's finally moved to her dream home. That was always her dream, but she held herself back from it because she didn't think her mum would approve. Before we worked together, she constantly put her mother's voice above her own. Not anymore!

Jessica completely changed her life once she started living on her own terms and connected to her huge heart. And she could do this because she got support and did the work to let go of identities that had never belonged to her in the first place, and that definitely weren't serving her.

YOUR WORD IS YOUR WAND (SO WATCH YOUR LANGUAGE)

A huge part of reframing your experiences and identity is looking at the language you use to describe them. One of my favorite quotes from Florence Scovel Shinn is "Your word is your wand".
She's not wrong - our words are the magic wands we use to cast spells of creation in our lives. Everything in your world starts with a thought, then turns into a word, then into an action, and finally becomes a tangible thing that you experience in your life.

Language creates our entire lives. Just take a moment to fully let that in.

"Whether you tell yourself you can do something or not... you're right."

– Henry Ford

So, if you describe a situation as too hard to manage, guess how it will feel to you whenever you try to deal with it. If you say you simply aren't capable of doing something, what do you think your chances of success are?

Here are just a few of the words you'll NEVER hear me use these days outside of this book. Why? Because I know how powerful this language is at bringing me the things I don't want:

- 'Hard' or 'struggle'.
- 'Block'.
- 'Can't'.
- 'Hope to' or 'try'.
- 'Don't know'.

These days, I'm incredibly intentional with my language. That's why I reach for powerful, positive words instead, like:

- 'Challenging' - I can overcome a challenge, and then feel a sense of achievement once I've conquered it.
- 'Obstacle' - again, I can get past an obstacle, but a 'block' stops me from moving forward.
- 'Can', or even better, 'WILL' - this one's probably self-explanatory, although see my note below about 'hope' and 'try'.
- 'I'll find out' / 'feel into' - 'don't know' is an endpoint, while these words give me a clear next action to take.

A NOTE ABOUT HOPING AND TRYING

When you look at the words above that I no longer use, you might notice that most of them have something in common. They're almost all negative, while the words I replace them with are positive.

All of them, that is, except for 'hope' and 'try'. So why are they the odd ones out? After all, having hope is supposed to be a good thing, isn't it? If we don't hold any hope of getting what we want in our lives, doesn't that mean we give up? And - like the old saying goes - isn't it better to have tried and failed than never to have tried at all?

NOPE!

Sorry to burst your bubble there, but 'hope' and 'try' aren't nearly as positive as they seem on the surface.
If you 'hope' for something, you're abdicating your power as the creator of your experiences. You're saying that whether or not you get the thing you want depends on someone or something else, and that you

have no control over the outcome.

The women who sign up for my programs so often tell me, "I really hope this works for me." And when they do, I immediately shut that idea down.

I tell them, "There's no such thing as hope in my Vortex. You get to choose whether this program will work for you or not. If you're 100% committed, it will work for you because it's a proven process - but YOU need to make the choice to commit and declare that this is the solution."

Similarly, if you 'try', you're not truly committing to, and putting your back into, getting what you want. It's a way of accepting from the start that you might not get it, then letting yourself off the hook in advance. There's a quality of claiming the outcomes you dream about in the energy of words like 'I am' or 'I will' that's totally absent from 'I'll try' or 'I hope to'.

So don't be fooled by the apparently positive nature of 'try' and 'hope'. They're stealth torpedoes that will punch holes in the ship of your dreams and sink it before it ever gets a chance to set sail.
In even simpler terms, it's like when someone says, "Oh, I'll try to come to your drinks." That response is flat-out lame. It leaves the door open for other options with zero commitment. They're either coming to the drinks, or they're not.

You know yourself that when you give that kind of response, you probably won't go. You just don't want to take responsibility for saying, "No," at the time.

CALLING IN MY SOULMATE SHOWED
ME HOW POWERFUL LANGUAGE WAS

Back when I first decided to attract my soulmate, I thought I was DOING all the right things. I kept putting myself out there, and I had no trouble at all getting dates.

The problem was that I didn't intentionally define the kind of dates I wanted. I wasn't using my words as my wand, and instead, I just thought, "Oh, cool, yay, another date. Yep, sure. I'll go out with him. Why not?"

I had no discernment around whether those dates took me in the direction I wanted to go, or whether I even actually liked the guy. So I sat in the back seat of my life, letting the dates just take me wherever. I basically handed my power over to the guy, which was a recipe for disaster.

Then I used to use super-low-vibrational language like:

- *"I always attract guys who refuse to show up for me."*
- *"Love is hard."*
- *"I'm not good at relationships or commitment. I don't think I'm built for them. I'm just a free spirit."*

I remember the exact moment I clocked that my word was my wand in relationships, just like it was in every area of my life. I suddenly realized that, holy shit, I'd been talking about all the things that weren't working... so guess what I kept seeing more of in my life? My language was literally tainting my new relationships with my conviction that love was hard.

Right then and there, I got intentional about using my words to create my ideal soulmate relationship. I picked a date, and told all my friends, "He's coming in by December 27, 2014 — three months from now." Every time I said this, I spoke from a very intentional place, but also one of excitement and light-hearted energy. Most importantly, I believed deep in my heart that he'd show up, and I put all my faith in the Universe to orchestrate the how.

My friends just looked at me as though I was batshit crazy. After all, I was doing an off-Broadway show at that point. I didn't look like I had TIME to attract in a new soulmate! Plus, I was also living in New York City, where everyone talks about how hard love is and how awful men are. So I just had to stop having those conversations. I had to stop complaining. And I had to stop hanging around anyone else who complained.

Instead, I only ever talked about what I did want. I told everyone how excited I was that this was going to happen. I celebrated how it was going to feel in advance. I made sure my language was intentional and left no room for doubt.

(And yes — of course — meanwhile, I continued to do all the things you'll learn to do in this book. I treasured myself and treated myself like a Queen. But without the container of my language, those actions just wouldn't have been enough.)

You already know the ending to this story. Anaam — my amazing soulmate — came right into my life, and before the date I'd set. Now, each night when we lie in bed together with his arms around me, I think back to the fun I had calling him into my Vortex.

I got intentional with my language, and the Universe responded by filling the order I'd put in for him.

I know it sounds a little cray, but if you want your soulmate to come into your life, you need to get with the program, sister! It's your time, and you totally deserve it. Use your language intentionally - to reflect your highest vibrational dreams, instead of your fears and frustrations. Then feel grateful for the absolute certainty that it's on its way.

The Universe responds to certainty. I knew what I wanted, spoke it out loud, felt it in every cell in my body, and then trusted the Universe to bring it to me. Period!

ALIGN YOUR ACTIONS WITH YOUR LANGUAGE

Of course, you can't just swap out a negative term in your language for a better one and suddenly expect the Universe to rearrange itself. The words you speak are the beginning of transformation, but they're far from the end. You need to climb into the front seat of your life and take control of everything in it, which means that your actions need to support your language.

When I called in my soulmate, I had to say, "OK, he'll be here in three months... so I now have three months to step up in my life." I knew that if I wanted to attract an amazing, grounded, healthy, awesome guy, I needed to be feeling good about myself when he got here. I needed to feel great in my own skin. I needed to feel amazing in my body, nourish myself and do all the things that brought me pleasure - like dancing, acting and spending time with supportive friends.

I also needed to start letting go of the behaviors that didn't serve me. I've already mentioned ditching the trash-talking: the complaining about previous dates or thinking of relationships as 'hard'.

But I was also acting in ways that weren't for my highest good, and that had to stop too. I'd go out binge-drinking with friends quite regularly. So I decided to get off the booze train, which was the best decision I ever made. I also had one or two comfortable, convenient 'friends-with-benefits' relationships that needed to go.

I realized that I needed to wake the fuck up. If my soulmate turned up while I was still going out on benders and having commitment-free flings, he and I would probably miss each other. So I had to let those incongruent behaviors go, and start acting like the Queen I truly was if I wanted him to recognize me when he arrived.

Now, you might not be quite the party girl I was back then. But I promise you: right now, you're acting in ways that just aren't congruent with the life you long for or the woman that you are. So yes, get intentional with your language and how you speak. But also make damn sure that your actions are congruent with your dreams and desires.

What does that mean? If you're seeing a guy who isn't showing up for you - NEXT! If you're with a married man and waiting for him to leave his wife for you - NEXT! Show some respect for yourself, darling. Take these jerks off the pedestal you've stuck them on, and pop yourself up there instead.

You can create literally anything you want in your life if you just honor your words with your actions and spend more time hanging out with your heart. That means getting quiet enough to ask your heart how it feels about everything in your life. Then listen for the answer.

Trust me, superstar: your heart will tell you every single time. You just need to get used to its cues, and that means striking up a relationship. But YOU'VE got to make the first move - your heart got tired of trying to communicate with you when you weren't listening a long time ago.

REFRAMES TAKE PRACTICE, BUT THEY CAN CHANGE YOUR LIFE

OK, so you understand that you're the creator of your life, and that nobody has the power to control your responses other than you. You get - at least intellectually - that nobody and nothing can affect you because you, my friend, no longer let people shit in your Vortex!

But if you're like many of my clients, you probably want to ask:
  · "Where do I go from here?"
  · "How do I remember to actually 'walk the walk' in my day-to-day life?"

- "How do I remind myself that I have the power to choose the frame I view my experiences through when I'm knee-deep in the thick of them?"

The answer is that it starts - as everything does - with a decision. So right now, I want you to declare that you deserve the life you dream of. If your deepest desire is to attract your soulmate, declare right now that you're lovable, beautiful and soulmate material. If you're dreaming of a particular lifestyle or business or bank balance, declare that you ARE someone who always gets what she asks for.

(Later, you'll need to build your belief muscle and start feeling into these words every day. For now, I just want you to make the decision, and let yourself get excited about being able to create this blueprint for yourself.)

Next, commit to aligning your language and your actions with that decision. And, super-importantly, commit to bringing yourself back on track whenever you stumble. Because - and I say this with love, beautiful woman - you will stumble. We all do.

We're all perfectly imperfect, and that means we mess up sometimes. It's all part of the process.

To (slightly mis)quote Vince Lombardi, **"It's not about whether you fall down or not. It's whether - and how quickly - you get back up again afterward."**

So don't make it into a big drama when you stumble. Don't make it mean anything huge and earth-shattering. Just have a little fun with it. Laugh at yourself. Find a friend who understands and tell her, "Oh my God, did you just hear me? I said the word 'try' five times in ten minutes! How crazy is that?"

Then recommit to using better, more powerful language instead from that moment forward. And keep recommitting, however many times it takes. Be kind to yourself as you do. And most importantly, be patient with yourself and your process. Don't get bogged down or berate yourself. Have fun with it. I promise that, eventually, you'll get addicted to it because you're going to start getting what you ask for!

It might come in a different way to what you expect, but the Universe is pretty damn clever. So when you ask and expect to receive, you will.

You don't second-guess the fish man when you ask for a piece of fish, and the Universe is no different. Yes, 'ask and you shall receive', but you also need to strengthen your belief muscle to create more certainty about whatever you ask for.

That's why, in the next chapter, we'll look at how to actually feel into and connect with the things you're saying, rather than just saying them. That's a trap that I see SO many women fall into - 'doing' self-development instead of allowing it in and feeling it. It's classic self-sabotage, so don't let that be you.

Supercharge your intentions by learning how to really feel. That will get you firing on all cylinders down your dream highway, baby. Wahooooooo!

BUDDY UP TO AMPLIFY YOUR REFRAME POWER

Before we move to the next chapter though, you might want to look outside of yourself for a little accountability and support.
I highly recommend finding a friend who's also invested in raising her vibration and creating through her Vortex. Ask if she'd like to play a game where you're both only allowed to talk about the things you WANT in your lives. You could even create a private WhatsApp group that you can each only use for your high-vibrational dream chats.

Once she agrees, commit to lovingly pulling each other up whenever you hear the other one use a disempowering word. You could also hold each other accountable for the actions you'll each take - or stop taking - to align with your new language. Then check in daily by text or on your WhatsApp group, or whatever works for you.

I did that with a friend, and we only ever shared about the awesome time we were each having with our respective men. We described what we did together with them, and how they made us each feel. The funny thing is that when I messaged her after finally meeting Anaam, she couldn't tell whether I was doing my dream work, or if it was real. That's how invested we both were.

AND IT WORKED!

This is the Law of Attraction in action. It's yours to use. Don't buy into your current circumstance. Speak into existence exactly what your heart longs to create, and then don't be surprised when it shows up!

THE GOLD NUGGETS

Beautiful woman, we've covered some gold together in the last few pages. Here's a quick recap of the 24-karat nuggets to take away with you and treasure as you head into the next chapter:

• You can view your experiences through many different frames of meaning - 'reframing' is the process of intentionally choosing a powerful meaning for something that feels shitty.

• You don't have to deny your authentic experiences, but you can change how you think - and speak - about them to allow yourself to fucking thrive.
• You can reframe more than just individual experiences - you can reframe your entire identity too.

• When it comes to reframing anything, your words are your wand: choose powerful, high-vibrational language that keeps you from shitting in your Vortex.

GIFT WORK

Over to you, superstar! In this chapter, you've journeyed through the power of the reframe and using your word as your wand. Now it's time to really bed that knowledge down to make it your new normal. Do this, and you'll change your life!

First, questions to journal about:

- How do you describe your life right now? Do you complain about things not working out, eg. in relationships?
- How often do you speak lovingly to yourself? Is it always, sometimes or never?
- What's the current story you're telling yourself about love (or whatever else you want to manifest in your life)?
- What do you want to replace that story with?

Next, join my free Facebook group, *Ignite Your Queen Attract Your Soulmate*. Find us at *www.facebook.com/groups/IgniteYourQueen* and start interacting with the wonderful women there. You might even find an accountability buddy too.

Finally, check out my Empress Morning Activation meditation on the book bonuses page at *www.soultosoulglobal.com/book-bonuses*. You can either listen to me guiding you through this meditation, or - even more powerfully - use the script on the page to record it in your own voice. Either way, listen to it first thing every morning to help you recommit to speaking and acting in alignment with your dream.

CHAPTER FIVE

The Intellectualizing Self-Development

TRAP

"The quicker you do the work, the quicker you'll be in alignment with your desires."

Great - you've changed the frame you view the world through. You've also changed your language and then aligned your actions with it. But there's still a little more to this transformation thing.

Many women come to me frustrated because they've spent years reading all the books, watching YouTube videos, doing their gratitudes, getting healings, taking ayahuasca trips to Peru... But despite all of this, they're still not getting results.

The problem is that they're outsourcing their inner work and relying on the things they're doing to change them. They're not taking responsibility for doing the work at a heart level themselves.

And so, spoiler alert: nothing ever changes. Here's how to avoid doing the same thing in YOUR life.

THE LESSER-KNOWN 'LAW OF DISTRACTION'

At one end of the spectrum, we have the women I've talked about above, who do all the healings and courses and self-development reading. And then, at the other end, I regularly see clients who try to outsource everything. They make a list of all the things they want - which, yes sure, is a great first move. But then they step back, write their gratitude list by rote each day, and 'wait for the Universe to make it happen'.

They'll often tell me, "Oh, I've put in my cosmic order. Now I'll wait for the Universe to bring me my ideal man." Or perhaps, "Yep, I know what I want my life to look like. Now it's up to the Universe to manifest my million-dollar business launch."

Meanwhile, they don't open their hearts. They just go through the motions in their heads, and intellectualize self-development with a checklist.

Look, the Universe is absolutely, 100% capable of sending them their soulmates and the juicy business opportunities they're dreaming of. But regardless of how many gratitudes they write, if they keep operating out of the same shitty frequency they've been doing up until now, I guarantee what they want won't show up. That's because they're sitting in a place of entitlement, and the Universe doesn't respond to that.

Manifestation and transformation are co-creations.

We have to get our inner 'ducks in a row' first to become vibrational matches for whatever we want to receive. These women aren't doing that, though. They're just stating what they want and then hoping for the best. Being lazy with their dreams is costing them precious time that they'll never get back.

To be fair, they - much like the clients who've done all the healings and courses - don't feel like they're being lazy. If I ask them, they'll tell me they're TOTALLY doing the work. They've read all this stuff about the Law of Attraction and focusing on the positive, and now they're committing full-out to 'good vibes only'.

Meanwhile, their shadow selves - their lower, limiting selves - make them feel hella uncomfortable. But they're all about the 'positive vibes' now, so they push the discomfort down and refuse to acknowledge it. After all, doesn't the Law of Attraction tell them that if they focus on something bad, they'll just attract more of it?

And yes, like I said in Chapter 2, I get the temptation to do that. I was so full of the shit I was ignoring that I didn't know which way was up. I kept burying my head in the sand, pretending all that stuff didn't exist. Meanwhile, I wrote down my gratitudes, made my vision boards and kept telling myself I was doing the work. It was a complete spiritual bypass - a way of turning 'the Law of Attraction' into 'the Law of Distraction'.

But my darling one, I wasted so much time. I seriously wish someone had hit me over the head with a big, fat saucepan and yelled, "For God's sake, WAKE THE FUCK UP, LUCY!" So if this chapter feels a bit like a slap across your knuckles, I'm totally OK with that. Because it's time to stop talking about what you want and start actually getting it.

In fact, if anything I'm saying here is deeply triggering you, that's fantastic. That triggered feeling is jolting you out of your comfortable, numb place of thinking and rationalizing in your head. It's forcing you to start acknowledging and experiencing your authentic feelings again.

And until you do that, sister, nothing - and no one, for that matter - can help you.

So if you're feeling triggered, celebrate the hell out of it. It means you're ready to start feeling again. You're ready to start facing your fears and insecurities and all those uncomfortable emotions you've been shoving deep down where you don't have to feel them.

And that means you're ready for real transformation.

I USED TO BE THE
QUEEN OF CONTRADICTION

I've talked already about how I used the Law of Distraction to keep from having to deal with my inner shit. But honestly, if I'd taken a good, hard look at how I was living my life, it would have been blatantly obvious that everything was NOT sunshine and rainbows in Lucy-land.

For example, I had the most beautiful – and I mean stunning – vision board imaginable sitting right where I could see it every day. (And I was pretty chuffed with myself for creating it). I kept my gratitude journal by my bedside, and I wrote list after list in it every single morning. I went to my weekly kinesiology sessions and basked in how clean, clear and totally 'high-vibe' it left me feeling.

BUT... in the minutes and hours and days between my healing sessions and my autopilot gratitude journaling? In those moments, I was a walking contradiction. I'd go out each evening with my friends and get completely obliterated at bars.

I did the same thing with my dates too. I'd tell the Universe I wanted to manifest this handsome, kind, spiritual, supportive soulmate. But then, when I went out on dates to meet this guy, what did I do? I got thoroughly trashed with my date for the evening.

It was like I was determined to undo all the wonderful effects the healing had created for my vibration. Cue the movie How to Lose a Guy in Ten Days! I took zero responsibility for how I was feeling or for changing any of the vibration-lowering habits in other areas of my life. So, not surprisingly, I attracted guys who mirrored that back to me.

And meanwhile, I put zero effort into self-love, AKA connecting with my heart, which is the power source for my Vortex.

Now, let me be clear here: 'self-love' isn't a mani-pedi or a luxury spa weekend. They're divine, of course, and they can be part of treating ourselves. But REAL self-love is about pouring love into the parts of ourselves that hurt. It's about being willing to look at those parts – to acknowledge them and stop numbing them with alcohol or drugs or food or anything else.

I couldn't see that at the time, though. I really thought I was being self-loving. I thought those booze binges were just me 'having a bit of fun till my soulmate gets here'. And if I started to catch a sideways glimpse of the contradiction I was embodying, I'd find a way to make it someone else's fault. I'd tell myself things like, "I'm a free spirit. It's just that the guys I connect with never get me..." Or occasionally, I'd fall back on the old, "Well, maybe I'm not soulmate material after all."

*It took a super-confronting session with a new mentor who cut straight through my crap to truly see how out of alignment my actions were. (And if you're looking for your own mentor, check out my masterclass in the book bonuses section of my website at **www.soultosoulglobal.com/book-bonuses**).*

When I finally realized that what I was doing wasn't working, I got the right support. I refused to let anything or anyone stop me. I went on a mission to step the fuck up. I could no longer tolerate my mediocre way of living, where I just accepted the same shit year after year. I was sick to death of not being the chosen one, living in Victim Village and never feeling like I was enough.

I realized that I needed to start genuinely loving myself. I had to see myself as the epic Queen that I was born to be. More than that, I had to start behaving like someone who fully saw herself as that person. That meant the drinking binges had to go. And yes, I had friends at the time who asked, confused, "But Lucy, how can you date if you're not going to drink?"

Once again though, I just smiled: I knew my soulmate would 100% support me when I acted in self-loving ways. And whaddya know? When Anaam and I had our first date, he said, "Oh, you don't drink? That's cool. I might just not drink with you."

Ding ding ding ding ding! That, right there, is the power of alignment.

When you're living in alignment, connecting to your heart and genuinely feeling your feelings, you'll KNOW it. That state feels juicy and delicious - like you're creating your dream life in every single moment. You'll feel like you're dancing with life, and you'll know on a deep, soul level that anything you imagine is possible.
Want more of that? Read on, beauty!

THE GOLD STANDARD TEST FOR JUDGING A TECHNIQUE

At this point, you might be wondering, *"OK, well if kinesiology and other forms of healing aren't effective, what is?"*
But that's NOT what I'm saying at all.

Kinesiology - and reiki, and Theta, and pretty much every other form of healing ever - absolutely can be effective, at least for some people. But they're only effective when they're one piece of the overall puzzle. They're not silver bullets that will magically change everything about your relationship with yourself and your past overnight.

The same is true of books and courses - assuming, of course, that you're actually putting what you learn into action. As we've discussed, if you just add what you read to the giant library of info circling around in your head, it won't do a freaking thing.
So how do you know whether a healing technique, book, course or whatever is working for you? It's simple: look at your life at that moment and ask yourself, *"Do I have what I want? Or am I still in the exact same place I was before?"*

Ignore how much time and money you've already invested in whatever the method is. Don't think about how much work you've already done - that's a classic roadblock to figuring out whether you should keep going with it or not.

(Don't believe me? Google the term 'sunk cost bias'. That's the official, academic name for our very human tendency to keep doing something that doesn't work because we don't want to waste the time and money we've already spent on it. It's like staying in the wrong relationship because you've already invested time and energy into it, and you're hoping it's going to magically get better someday.)

Instead of focusing on all those things, take a step back and look long and hard at yourself from the outside. Ask yourself, *"Right now, am I attracting higher-caliber men than I was before or not?"* or *"Right now, am I living the lifestyle I wanted to manifest or not?"*

And sister, please don't tell me that whatever you're doing is, "... starting to work for you, but just needs more time." It's my life's mission to call bullshit on everyone who insists that transformation has to be a long, painful, drawn-out process that takes years and years. That's utter crap, and you're way too smart for the slow road.

So if you've been doing the same thing for months or even years, and you're still not where you want to be? Then, divine woman, it is long past time to admit that it's not working. It's time to get the right support from someone who inspires you and has already walked the path before you.

HOW MUCH LONGER CAN YOU ACCEPT NOTHING CHANGING?

When Naomi came to me, she'd been doing self-development for ten years, and had been single for twelve. Most of that had been trying to do it all herself: reading books, watching YouTube videos, listening to podcasts and doing occasional workshops. She'd also grown up believing that vulnerability was weak, and that getting support would mean she was a failure.

What I most noticed on our breakthrough call together was how many times she used the word 'try' to describe her self-development efforts. (Remember talking about 'try' in Chapter 4?) She had no plan, no structure and no mentor. So I called her out on it and asked her what had made her book the call.

She replied that she couldn't go one more day trying to figure it out on her own. She was numb. She'd been trying to do everything herself for ten freaking years and clearly, nothing had changed.

So I explained that she'd been doing self-development intellectually. She wasn't feeling and connecting to those parts of her that were numb. And she couldn't un-numb and clear 30+ years of conditioning by watching a YouTube video.

The instant Naomi started my Soul to Soul program, she felt the shift. She felt supported in a way she'd never felt before in her life. She felt seen and safe to get messy and vulnerable. And for the first time, she saw clearly how much she'd been living in her head instead of her heart.

Once Naomi started to really FEEL, she was unstoppable. She got a taste of who she was born to be and began to fall head-over-heels in love with herself. It was like she'd lit a fire inside of her soul, and she felt shocked at how much she'd been holding back. This extended to every area of her life, but especially her true expression.

Today, Naomi has aligned with her greatness and has set out on her true path, which is healing animals. She'd been making excuses for avoiding it and been too scared to commit to it before. But during the program, she vowed that she'd never let anyone or anything hold her back from her desires again.

She now feels like a rockstar in her skin and is ready to take up as much space in the world as she can. And best of all, she knows that she can create whatever she puts her heart and mind to.

Important note: you might be reading this and beating yourself up, thinking, *"OMG, I've also wasted ten years of my life reading self-help books to fix myself, and nothing's changed. I must have so much baggage that I'll never get over it!"*

If so, I want you to stop that shit this instant!

Firstly, nothing you do is ever wasted. There are also plenty of things that have helped you along the way, so make them count. Go the extra mile with them. Don't be one of those women who give up just before

M DONE.

they reach the pot of gold.

Don't look back. Keep looking forward, gorgeous.

The only moment you can control in your life is right NOW.

Secondly, you can't do anything about your past choices. Beating yourself up over them just means you're focusing on the past, instead of doing something now about your future. Remember that there's nothing wrong with you. You've just been feeding the wrong story and focusing on your trauma and your not-enough-ness instead of your power.

And right now, you get to make a different choice. You get to choose whether your response to becoming aware of it is, "That's not possible - nothing will ever help me!" or *"Oh, thank fuck there's a better way of doing this that will genuinely change things!"*

Which option will you choose?

IT'S TIME TO GET OUT OF YOUR HEAD AND INTO YOUR HEART

I've talked a lot in this book about 'doing your gratefuls', and it might sound like I'm saying you shouldn't keep a gratitude list. But that's totally not true - regular gratitude journaling is incredibly powerful IF you do it right.

And when I say 'incredibly powerful', I mean it can immediately shift you into a state of joy in the present. That's the state the Law of Attraction most responds to. Doing gratitude right can fast-track you into your soulmate relationship - or whatever else you want to create in your life. It's your fastest train out of Victim Village. And, if you do it right, it can even detox your Vortex.

Unfortunately though, if you approach gratitude the way I used to - on autopilot, as just another task on your to-do list - it'll never be anything more than a checked box for you. You'll be filling your Vortex with a life on autopilot, too.

88

Don't you think you've had enough of that, beauty?

So what's the 'right' way to approach gratitude? You need to get out of your head, where you think intellectually and rationally about what you can (or maybe even should) be grateful for. Instead, you drop down into your heart and feel into what you truly ARE grateful for.

One of the most fun parts about gratitude - the part my clients and I both love - is the 'future gratefuls'. You can use this for anything you want to attract into your life: your soulmate, new opportunities, a new home, a baby, whatever. Here's how...
Close your eyes, put your hands over your heart, and connect to your beautiful Vortex. Then, open your eyes, write down each 'grateful' and feel it deep in your bones. Let yourself sink into the amazing feeling of already having it in your life. Let it move you.

Before I had my baby girl, I did future 'gratefuls' about what it felt like to have her in my arms and breastfeed her. And it brought me to happy tears every single time I did it. I also did future 'gratefuls' about her birth and hearing her crying loudly as the nurse handed her to me, so I knew she was healthy. That's what happened in real life. She was born a super-healthy baby with the loudest cry to let mummy know all was well.

It's just so powerful to do this every day. The only thing you need to remember is to FEEL each 'grateful' you write with every fiber of your being before you move to the next one.

You can write out a set number if you want to: I like to write ten a day. OR sometimes, I record them on my phone, then close my eyes and listen so I feel like I'm chatting directly with the Universe. Sometimes, it's fun to play back one of my pre-recorded 'gratefuls' if I'm on the go. I'll just pick one that I loved and marked on my phone as a goody.

I love to mix up the formats for my 'gratefuls', but just do what feels best for you. As long as you FEEL them every day, that's all that matters. You'll definitely see results, and you won't want to miss a day. (Plus, it also has incredible benefits for your nervous system and health. Double win!)

Another amazing way of doing your 'gratefuls' properly is being grateful for the obstacles you've encountered along the way. When you're grateful for what an obstacle teaches you, it'll dissolve a lot faster than if you spiral around in frustration and 'why me?' energy.

Do it. I promise that you'll wish you'd had this trick up your sleeve a long time ago.

This is like the advanced PhD level of gratitude. *Anyone* can feel grateful for the obviously wonderful things they experience (although it's disturbing how many people seem determined not to!) But it takes a special kind of willingness to be authentically grateful for things that haven't happened yet, and for obstacles and challenges.

So when you feel like there's nothing there to be grateful for, or when the obstacles and curveballs of life make it challenging to connect with gratitude in your heart, ask yourself:

· *"What could be good about this situation?"*
· *"Since everything is rigged in my favor, what is this teaching or showing me?"*
· *"Where's the gold in this obstacle?"*

Trust me: the results will be nothing short of miraculous.
OK, so now you've got a handle on how to avoid surface-level self-development. You know how to do the deep, nitty-gritty work of getting into your heart and radiating gratitude into your Vortex. Now it's time to dive in and explore what your Vortex REALLY is, how it works and how to keep it vibrating at its highest possible level.

That's what we're doing in the next chapter!

THE GOLD NUGGETS

Beautiful woman, we've covered some gold together in the last few pages. Here's a quick recap of the 24-karat nuggets to take away with you and treasure as you head into the next chapter:

• It doesn't matter how much self-development work you've done - if you're not seeing results externally in your life, you're not doing the right work.

• You might be in denial about this the way I was, using books, healings and courses to distract yourself from the real work you need to do.

• Commit like a rockstar to FEELING your 'gratefuls' instead of doing them on autopilot - for epic results, align, commit, feel and repeat.

GIFT WORK

Over to you, superstar! Are you ready to dive in and actually feel so you can attract in the life of your dreams? Then let's get going! Here are some things you can do to do just that:

Journaling is key, so every morning, write a list of ten 'future gratefuls' that light your soul on fire.

- Connect with your heart before you do them, and then again after you write them.
- Spend time consciously connecting with your Vortex and feeling grateful today for them already being in your life.
- Feel that gratitude with every cell in your body, then let go and let

your imagination take over!
Also, ask yourself how this higher version of you would show up for
herself right now. Think about the version of yourself that's already in
a soulmate relationship, living on purpose and thriving in her life. Then
ask:

- How does she think?
- How does she feel in her soul?
- What is her level of commitment to herself?

Next, ask yourself how you can align your actions with your intentions
and your energy with your desires. In your journal, list the areas you
need to clean up to get into alignment. This is about already living,
breathing and being this highest version of yourself today.

Finally, get obsessed with your JOY, knowing that joy puts you into
receiving mode.

- Go and do something right now that gets you super-LIT, excited
  and in your happy zone. It could be as simple as feeding the ducks
  or dancing naked around your living room to high-vibrational
  music.
- Then make sure you prioritize your daily doses of joy. They'll keep
  you plugged into your Vortex and in your limitless epicenter of
  creation.

CHAPTER SIX

The Care and Feeding of your

VORTEX

"Prioritize time every morning for your download with the Divine."

So now you understand why the way you feel, think and speak affects your reality. You also know how to choose what you make experiences mean and reframe them. And you've learned how to tell when you're looking after your Vortex: everything seems to flow, and you have a sense of dancing with life.

Now it's time to get practical. Let's talk about what taking care of your Vortex looks like in practice. Plus, how do you stop people from shitting in it, and make damn sure you don't shit in it yourself?

YOU'VE CREATED EVERYTHING IN YOUR LIFE BY ALLOWING IT

Everything you experience comes from what you've allowed or disallowed.

Now there's a confronting statement if ever I've heard one. As we've already covered, shitty things DO happen in life. And whether you think they're just random events, or whether you believe you chose them in some karmic way, that's totally up to you.

At a base level though, why they happen doesn't matter. What does matter is that you get to choose how you react, and the meaning you make of those things.

Plus, yes, OK, sometimes shitty, apparently random things happen. But all too often, what creates your day-to-day reality is not just allowing, but sometimes actively inviting other people to take a big ol' dump in your Vortex. When you're out of alignment with Source energy (AKA with yourself and the Universe), you drop into icky, negative space. Once you're there, it's incredible how fast negativity breeds.

This gap is where you invite in everything you don't want. And THAT's when other people swoop in and shit in your Vortex. Now, depending on who you are, that might look like several different things. It might look like:

- Getting a phone call from that friend with an addiction to drama, who can't stop sobbing about her latest breakup (of many).
- Asking for opinions on a lifestyle change you want to make from that negative family member who knows nothing about the situation.
- Saying nothing while an acquaintance tells you all the reasons why the goal you're dreaming of could never possibly work.
- Climbing into a taxi with a racist driver who insists on ranting about the recession, and how it's all 'those people's faults'!

Now, while all of these situations might look like someone else doing something to you, I'm here to tell you, beauty, that every single one is you ALLOWING that experience. You're not enforcing - or even setting - any kind of boundary with those people to stop them from shitting in your Vortex. And that means leaving yourself wide open to their shit, with no boundaries to shut it out.

It's your responsibility, not theirs, to know what your boundaries are and to communicate them clearly. So if you just go ahead and listen to that person - if you give them that space in your mind and your heart and your Vortex? Then that is totally, completely and 100% on you.

In other words, you need to be discerning about who and what you allow into your Vortex. And if there's someone or something you don't want in there, you need to take responsibility for keeping them out.

Otherwise, you'll continue to feel exhausted, depleted, discouraged - and most importantly, no closer to your dream life.

HOW 'SHITTING IN YOUR VORTEX' AFFECTS YOUR REALITY

The most basic way to describe the Law of Attraction is that like attracts like. Through the magnetic power of your thoughts, you create your reality... and that can be both good and bad. Essentially, you get what you focus on, and the Universe is listening 24/7 without discriminating.

If you allow shitty thoughts, feelings and conversations into your Vortex, you'll create shitty results.

Imagine those thoughts, feelings and conversations as being like the food you put into your body. I'm not here to shame anyone for their diet, but you can't deny that when you eat good, fresh, whole food, your body feels fantastic and operates at the highest level, right? And when you eat a load of sugary, processed, greasy rubbish, you wake up the next morning feeling like crap with brain fog.

You need to be discerning about the food you allow into your body. You need to eat more of the stuff that nourishes you, and less of the crap. And you need to do EXACTLY the same for your Vortex - that's how you keep a clean, high-vibrational relationship with your mind.

In practice, this is about you taking control of your mind. It's about choosing your thoughts powerfully, instead of being a prisoner of your mind. It's about refusing to be negative or get sucked into other people's low-vibrational stories and language.

I used to listen to friends and acquaintances complaining about how tough dating and relationships were because I wanted to be a good friend. I wanted to lend a sympathetic ear. But - surprise, surprise - the more I listened to them complaining, the more I made their complaints my own story. And the worse my love life seemed to get.

Then, one day, I realized that I was actively inviting that negativity into my experience. I was throwing shit into my Vortex without being discerning about whether I wanted the shit in there or not. That was when I knew I had to start taking control of what I allowed into that sacred creation space.

YOU DON'T GET WHAT YOU DESERVE…

Have you ever looked at a situation in your life and said, "I don't deserve this kind of crap," or looked at a relationship and said, "I deserve SO much better"?

If so, then sister, I'm about to drop another truthbomb on you!

As far as the Universe is concerned, there's no such *thing* as 'deserving'. Yep, it's true. When it comes to bringing that gorgeous soulmate - or anything else - into your life, 'what you deserve' is irrelevant. That means:

- It doesn't matter what's on your resumé.
- It doesn't matter what your job title is.
- It doesn't matter how much you weigh.
- It doesn't matter which school you went to.
- It doesn't matter where, or how often, you've traveled.
- It doesn't matter how much personal development work you've done.

Seriously. None of that shit is relevant to the results you create in your life. I mean, there's nothing wrong with any of those things - they're all fantastic - but they have nothing to do with you being able to attract in the love of your life.

We don't get what we deserve. We get what we expect.

Just stop for a second, close your eyes and fully let that in. It's going to completely shift how you perceive your life right now. Your heartfelt, deep-down expectations about any situation will supercharge everything else in your Vortex, for better or worse.
So let's say that you're a high-powered executive (as a lot of my clients

are) with cover-girl looks who jets off to the Maldives every year (PS -
you go, girl!)

Then let's then say that you have a ton of people telling you what a
great catch you are. You have no doubt in your mind that you 'deserve'
a great relationship with a soulmate who really gets you.
Well, I hate to break it to you, but all of that is irrelevant. It's
meaningless unless you believe deep in your heart that you're worthy
of a soulmate relationship. It's not about intellectual 'deserve-ability'
on paper. It's a feeling in your heart.

And there's no gray area: you either fully believe or you don't.
So many of my clients come to me flat-out confused. They tell me,
"Lucy, I just don't get it! I have so much going for me... but I can't keep
a man to save myself!"

What's really going on underneath all of those accolades is a library-
worth of unacknowledged stories about how love never works out in
the end. And there are so many different scenarios as to why.

Some of those women saw their parents' relationships fail. Others
watched their parents fighting more times than they could count. Still
others have been through a series of bad relationships where the guy
always lets them down, and now they can't trust themselves OR men.
Some have friends who keep insisting - loudly and often - that men are
all alike and are only after one thing.

The bottom line is that deep down, in their heart of hearts, none of
these women expect their soulmates to turn up. And even if he does
show up, somewhere inside themselves, they expect everything to
quickly go to hell in a handbasket. Because as far as they're concerned,
men don't choose them, and it ALWAYS ends up falling apart, no matter
how hard they try.
If any of these stories are true for you, then regardless of how much
external validation you have for your 'deserve-ability', do you genuinely
think you'll manifest that soulmate you dream of? (If so, I'd suggest
going back and re-reading the last few chapters.)

We never get what we deserve. We only ever get what we expect. So whatever your goal is, if you're caught up in using external 'worthiness measures' - getting degree after degree or running marathon after marathon to prove your worth - I invite you to take a step back. Drop down deep into your heart and ask yourself:

- *"Do I actually believe that what I want will work out for me? Or do I believe that good things don't happen to me?"*
- *"Do I really believe that I can experience love? Or do I feel like the one that men never choose?"*
- *"Do I genuinely feel like the chosen one who's destined to have love in my life? Or do I feel like someone who's constantly disappointed and let down by love and life?"*

Look, I know these questions are confronting, but I'm rooting for you to get to the truth. The minute you do, you can create what you truly want. Not only that, but these answers will show you what's really going on in your Vortex at the moment, regardless of how much you might think you deserve something.

YOU ATTRACT WHO YOU ARE

I know I've talked a LOT about the 'before's and 'after's of my life when it came to calling in my soulmate. I've talked about my party-girl lifestyle, and how I had to wake up and take a good look at who I was being before I could even start to make space for him in my life. But this concept is so incredibly important that I think it's well worth repeating.

I remember at one point just before I had my wake-up call, my mum turned to me and said, "Lucy, you keep doing the same thing, time after time, and expecting a different result. You go to the same bar with your friends, stay up till all hours, drink far too much, and feel like crap the next day. You're certainly not winning in the love department. How on earth do you expect a different result?"

It hit me hard when Mum said that, because she was absolutely spot on. The definition of insanity is doing the same thing over and over again and expecting a different result... and that was exactly what I was doing.

I kept on not being discerning about who I went out with. I kept on not being discerning about what I did while I was out – how much I drank or who I kissed.

And so my life at that time was – not to put too fine a point on it – a shit show on repeat. Then I looked around at these drop-kick men I was attracting into my life, and I realized that the one common denominator amongst them was ME. I didn't believe deep down that love was safe. I didn't believe I was worthy of it. I was actually terrified of letting love in, and I didn't even know it.

> *So all the actions, thoughts and feelings I put into my Vortex made damn sure I only attracted guys I could get drunk and have fun with. Guys who were crap at committing. I'd never stopped long enough to take that in before. I just thought that was how it was meant to be for me.*
>
> *I had to change how I showed up before I stood any chance of transforming that. If I wanted to attract someone who was looking for the kind of serious, committed, epic soulmate relationship I dreamed of, I had to completely change who I was being.*

KEEPING YOUR VORTEX SHIT-FREE REQUIRES DISCERNMENT

I've used the word 'discernment' several times in this chapter. Let's talk a bit about what I mean by it, especially when it comes to the people and things you want to allow into your Vortex.

Discernment isn't a complicated concept. It just means getting intentional and deliberate about two things:

1. What you do and don't want in your life, and therefore...
2. What you will and won't allow into your Vortex.

It really is that simple. It's about stepping back and asking yourself, *"Do I want this thing in my Vortex or not?"*

If something's taking you closer to your dreams and desires, it's going to feel good. In that case, yes, allow that stuff into your Vortex. If it doesn't feel good, on the other hand, and it's taking you further away from what you want, recognize that.

Then DO something about it.

There's just one exception to this, which is (you guessed it) that if your pain is surfacing, it won't feel good in the moment. But the only way to deal with that pain is to look it square in the face and FEEL it and reframe it. Only then can you release it out of your Vortex and create a fresh slate that you can manifest what you DO want from. Be loving with yourself when you're working with that unresolved pain though, divine woman.

Let's revisit that example we talked about earlier with the racist cab driver who won't shut up about the recession. When you're sitting there in that taxi, it might feel like he's got all the power - but it's your choice to keep listening or not. You can keep letting him take that giant dump in your Vortex... or you can say, "Look, excuse me, Mr Cabbie, but I need to put my earphones in now. I'm here if you want to talk about possibilities, but otherwise, I've got other things I need to listen to."

(Or if you don't quite have the courage for that kind of confrontation yet, you could just say, "Sorry, I've got to listen to something on my phone now. Please excuse me!")

Bottom line: you need to be discerning about the words you speak into existence and fill your Vortex with, because your language creates your life. Remember that your word is your wand. You're either using it powerfully to create a powerful life, or using low-vibrational language to create a low-vibrational life.

As we talked about in the last chapter, if you keep saying that something's hard or that you, "... just don't know if you can do something," you're throwing a giant heap of shit into your Vortex. But if you open yourself up to possibility and say something like, "I'm not sure how I'll do it, but I know I'm going to make it happen," you're transforming that potential shit into gold.

I remember the first time I got intentional about the soulmate I wanted. I set a non-negotiable boundary that he couldn't be a smoker or a big drinker. I knew that smoking depletes your life force, and big drinkers are numbing something deep down. And I just didn't want anyone in my Vortex who was willing to do that to themselves.

IT'S ALL ABOUT BOUNDARIES

Once you've discerned what you do and don't want in your Vortex, you need to be willing to take action to keep the shit you don't want out. And that, my darling one, requires you to unapologetically set and maintain clear, powerful boundaries.

Imagine you had a newborn baby. You wouldn't allow just anyone near her, right? You wouldn't allow random people to play with her. Absolutely not! If someone had a cold, you wouldn't allow them to come near her developing immune system and sneeze all over her. And you certainly wouldn't allow a sketchy-looking stranger to pick her up.

Instead, you'd set a firm boundary around who could and couldn't come near her - who could and couldn't touch her. And you'd get all fierce mama bear toward anyone who didn't respect those boundaries.

Well, you need to treat yourself with exactly the same amount of loving protection and respect. You need to keep anything and anyone with even slightly sketchy energy well away from your Vortex. You need to fill it with beautiful, nourishing, high-vibrational ideas the same way you'd nourish and cuddle that baby if she were crying. And if that means you need to bless and release people out of your life so you can only surround yourself with the good ones, so be it.

I know it can feel sad letting people go. But if they aren't adding to your life, they're sucking your positive energy away like a vampire. They're also stopping all the awesome new people who could actually support you from coming into your life.

Sometimes, the Universe will do a lot of the heavy lifting for you. When you start to feel better and better, you'll raise your frequency and vibration. Those people won't know what's shifted, but they just won't be as drawn to you because you'll suddenly be on a different wavelength. Other times, you'll need to take responsibility for being unavailable for people that you know will bring your energy vibration down.

I want you to know that this is not about refusing to be a good friend to someone who has your back and adds value to your life. Of course you can be there for those people when they need your support... BUT you still need to set healthy boundaries.

And I promise that some people will come to mind as being there for you when things aren't going well, but don't like it when they are... If you're thinking of someone like that right now, you definitely need to bless and release them. Namaste, energy vampire!

One way to do this that feels good is to first energetically send them love and wish them nothing but the best. Then commit to just not being available for their shitty stories. Express your boundaries clearly. If your friends don't respect those boundaries, stop taking their calls. Don't hang out with them. There's no way around this. Why?

> *"We are the sum of the five people we*
> *hang around most."*
>
> — *Jim Rohn*

Remembering that should help you to make the right decision next time an energy vampire starts heading in your direction. You are NOT available, got it?

(Handy hint: you're going to need to get REALLY good at blessing and releasing people from your life on your journey to living your dream. Why not start getting some practice in now?)

SET YOUR BOUNDARIES, THEN BACK YOURSELF BY MAINTAINING THEM

Having boundaries is about having such deep reverence for yourself that you refuse to tolerate anything that's not aligned with them. It's about deeply honoring yourself... but you must also be willing to follow through.
So once you've decided on what you want, and what you will and won't allow, you need to be prepared to hold that boundary. That starts with giving yourself permission to have life on your terms. Just take a second to let that land, beautiful one. It's a radical shift in belief

systems, I know - you might even need to give yourself a quiet moment or two to truly take it in.

But without fully accepting it, you won't be prepared to take the action that's necessary to create and maintain your boundaries. And that means you won't get to deliberately create the future you dream of. You'll just keep doing what you've always done, and nothing will change.

To start setting boundaries, look at your life and notice where things don't feel aligned with how you want them to be.

Ask yourself:

- *"Am I genuinely happy with the way things are in this situation?"*
- *"If not, what do I want to happen instead?"*

So ask yourself, *"Do I love this job I'm doing?"* If the answer isn't a "Hellz, yes!" take a little time to come out of your head. Drop into your heart and ask it, "What would you like me to do?" Then wait and see if anything comes up.

If it doesn't, don't sweat it - but keep checking in every morning. I promise it'll come to you.

Or perhaps your question might be, *"Do I actually like the way this friend treats me?"* If the answer's a 'No', allow yourself to get honest about how you'd like it to be instead.

Maybe YOUR question is, *"Am I honestly happy for my mum to constantly call at every hour of the day and night, depleting my energy with her negativity?"* If the answer's a 'No', what do you want instead?

The answers you get to those questions might show you that you need to tweak things in your life. Because of this, I want you to change the way you see yourself and your relationship to boundaries. Successful people know that having firm boundaries is the only possible way to thrive. Meanwhile, many people who aspire to be successful burn out along the way. They over-give and become exhausted because their boundaries are weak, if they have any at all.

So start relating to yourself as someone with epic, super-firm boundaries. It's time to channel your inner superhero and step right into that identity. Choose a superhero identity that inspires you for yourself. (Mine is Captain Marvel. She doesn't tolerate any crap, and I keep her figurine on my desk to remind me every day to step into my superhero identity. Trust me: it helps a lot.)

Whoever you choose, every morning when you wake up, intentionally step into their identity. See yourself as someone with strong boundaries, and you'll very quickly start to soar in every area.

It's important to acknowledge that this isn't about being rigid. If your friend has just been given a serious health diagnosis, it's OK to let yourself be there for her. But for both of your sakes, you still need to put some boundaries around HOW you show up for her.

Maybe you could say, "Hey, I know that's really scary to hear. I've got 20 minutes right now where I can give you my full, undivided attention. I can listen to what you're going through and comfort you, whatever you need, but then I'll have to hop off the call." You'll find that the conversation you end up having after you set a clear boundary will give your friend far more value than if you let it go on for hours.

But that's a very different situation to that one friend who always calls with a new drama of the week that she wants to pull you into. And again, you need to develop the discernment to figure out the right way to respond to each one.

One last thing about boundaries, beauty. If you clearly communicate your boundaries to someone who refuses to respect them or doesn't align with them, that tells you everything you need to know about them. You might find yourself wanting to make an exception or excuses for them. If so, nip that shit in the bud. You're not serving your friend by letting them cross your boundaries. You sure as hell aren't getting yourself closer to your dream. It's just enabling behavior that comes from lack.

I'M DONE.

I knew one woman who set the same boundary I did around refusing to have a relationship with a smoker. But then, when she met a guy she liked, she wouldn't back herself. She rationalized it by saying, "Oh, well at least he's only smoking. He could be doing heroin."

And I said, "Are you fucking kidding me? That's like saying, 'At least he only talks shit to me. He could be physically assaulting me.'"

Trust me: adapting your standards to someone else means completely dishonoring yourself. It means stepping on your dream, and diluting what you want for fear of losing someone who wasn't actually aligned with you in the first place.

Again, bless and release those people. Let them go, and feel grateful that they're just not part of your journey anymore.

SETTING BOUNDARIES CAN TAKE
A SHITLOAD OF COURAGE

One of my clients, Fiona, was a beautiful, bright woman who had a relationship that felt... mostly OK when she first contacted me. Like so many of the women who get in touch with me, she thought it just needed a minor tweak here or there.

So she was pretty freaking shocked, ten minutes into the call, when I told her that the women I went on to work with were nearly all single... So if she wanted to work with me, she needed to break up with this guy. Only then would she have room to invite her real soulmate into her life.

I swear, she nearly had a panic attack on the call when I dropped the truthbomb on her: everything she said showed me she had zero boundaries or self-worth. But she had no idea how unhappy she truly was because she'd never questioned her relationship.

I told her in no uncertain terms that if her relationship was perfect except for this, that or the other thing, then it WASN'T perfect.

Well, it took her a few days to come to terms with that, but once she did, she was all in. She broke up with the guy, and everything changed in her life once she did.

It wasn't just her relationship with guys – although that transformed dramatically. Where men used to treat her like a commodity, they started respecting her. In fact, a man in a position of power at her office who'd always dismissed her in the past suddenly started wanting to get to know her and asking for her opinion.

Meanwhile, her relationship with her mother – which had always been rocky – also improved. Where her mum had constantly talked down to Fiona and belittled her beliefs and life choices, she also now spoke to Fiona with a newfound respect.

It took Fiona a shitload of courage to start valuing herself enough to put those boundaries in place. But once she did, she clearly communicated to everyone in her life that she was done with allowing them to treat her like shit.

Now, you might think you've got your boundaries down pat, your Vortex is super-clear, and you're riding high with only one problem (He's not here yet, is he?) But there's one thing that nearly every woman I work with trips up on. And that's refusing to acknowledge that deep down, she's terrified of love.

I can't wait to dive deep into that with you in the next chapter.

THE GOLD NUGGETS

Beautiful woman, we've covered some gold together in the last few pages. Here's a quick recap of the 24-karat nuggets to take away with you and treasure as you head into the next chapter:

· Remember that your Vortex is your center of creation, so you need to spend time taking care of it and consciously creating from within it every day.

· You always, always, always get what you expect, not what you deserve.

• You are 100% responsible for everything you allow into your Vortex, even if they're things you don't want.

• You protect your Vortex from other people shitting in it by setting and enforcing clear boundaries.

• Maintaining boundaries takes courage, practice and action, but it's absolutely worth it - without them, you can't create from your highest vibration.

GIFT WORK

Over to you, superstar! Caring for and connecting with your Vortex is the essential ingredient in creating your dream life and attracting your soulmate. Get familiar with the points below to supercharge your energy.

First, make sure you devote some time first thing each morning to sit in your Vortex and connect with your big, juicy dreams. Letting your imagination run wild with your dream is super-elevating and only needs to take around four minutes.

Set your alarm, and if you go over that, it's a good thing. Listen to the Empress Morning Activation (find it on the book bonuses page at _www. soultosoulglobal.com/book-bonuses_) to charge you up, sister!

Next, create a powerful boundary by blessing and releasing. Let's give it a whirl right now, shall we?

Start by closing your eyes and putting your hands over your heart. Now, think of someone that you know deep down has been shitting in your Vortex.
Let yourself feel however you feel about how they've been stealing

your good energy from you... Let the feelings build, and really connect with those emotions. Some of them won't be pretty. They might have quite a strong charge. If so, that's good: don't go soft. Let your inner badass help you here.

Now feel yourself and your heart expanding. Feel your throat opening, and the ickiness melting away. Send a big ball of pink energy to their heart from yours - make it a nice, soft rose-quartz pink. Let that person know you love them, but that you're releasing them with love and sending high vibrations their way to sort themselves out.

Now repeat after me: "I am no longer available for people to shit in my Vortex. I deeply love and respect myself. I deeply love and honor my new, powerful boundaries. I deeply honor my own boundaries with myself. It's not my responsibility to rescue my friends and family. It IS my responsibility to put myself and my own needs first so I can share my love from a healthy place. I'm not responsible for anyone except for me. Me, first, now and forever. I love, adore and accept myself on every level. And so it is."

Take a deep breath and open your eyes. Light some sage if you have some, or even just light a match to clear the energy, and know that it is done.

CHAPTER SEVEN

Love
TERRIFIES ME

*"There is no greater power than
the energy of love."*

Have you noticed that, even though you know what your Vortex is and how to use it... something in your life still isn't working for you? Does it feel like you're stuck on a hamster wheel, doing the same old, same old and dating drop-kick men? If so, then beautiful one, you NEED to get a grip on what's really happening underneath the surface.

To help, in this chapter, I'll take you right down deep to where your abandonment and your fear live. These are the real reasons you don't currently have love in your life. I'll also introduce you to your inner little girl: that part of you that wants to protect you above all else.

It doesn't matter if you've already done a lot of intellectual 'little girl' work with a therapist or self-help book. Until you've truly healed her and made her feel seen, loved and valued, your King can't come into your life. Instead, he'll keep hovering around your Vortex, waiting for you to get this sorted, because he wants you in your Queen energy and your divine feminine power.
Ready? All right, let's rock!

WHY DON'T I HAVE LOVE?

The bottom line is that you don't have love right now because it fucking terrifies you. Otherwise, right in this moment, you'd already have the soulmate relationship you dream of in your life. You'd be thriving. That's the first truth I want you to let in, because the minute you can let it in, you can transform it.

You're also going to keep hearing me refer to the 'little girl' who's living inside of you in this chapter. That's because she's the one running the show, and she's the one blocking you from experiencing love. Whether you're in your 20s, 30s, 40s, 50s, 60s (all the way up to 100), there's one dominant energy hijacking your relationships. And that, divine woman, is your inner little girl.

Each time you hear me mention her, it might feel repetitive. But she's such a huge part of why love isn't working for you, so we need to get straight to the heart of this. That's the only way to get you out of singledom and into being the chosen one.

If your little girl is in charge of your Vortex, you're not going to attract your soulmate. Nor will you be fulfilled deep in your soul the way you're yearning to be. And that, beauty, is NOT OK.

You deserve the very best, so I'm gonna do everything in my power to help you get it. But you've got to work with me, because remember: this is a co-creation. That means no stubborn tricks or dabbling and doing the bare minimum, OK? Commit fully, take my lead and let's get your Queen on.

What's my little girl got to do with it?

So many women who come to me are confused as to why love isn't sticking. They ask:

- *"What's wrong with me?"*
- *"Why does it always fizzle?"*
- *"Why does he never turn out to be 'the one'?"*

It's not the man, my darling. It's you. It's your fear. I want you to admit, right in this moment, that love absolutely terrifies you. It doesn't feel safe. You're petrified of letting it in, of getting it wrong, of making the wrong decision. Deep down, you feel like a burden - so of course, that's showing up in your relationships too.
On top of that, you're constantly worrying, *"What if I choose the wrong guy?"* You don't feel enough for, or worthy of, a good

relationship. So the instant you do let love in, you're constantly afraid of him discovering the real you, and you slip straight into sabotage. You start pushing him away because you think he's just going to walk anyway, and you'd rather beat him to it. You can't see the point of letting someone in.

And *that's* where the revolving door of 'nothing ever working out for you' is born.

It's all because your inner little girl doesn't believe that love is safe. She doesn't believe that love works out for her. She expects it to end. And that's why it always does. Can you see now why dealing with your little girl is so damn important?

What's also going on at a very deep level is that you're terrified of being abandoned. That sense of abandonment comes from an experience when you felt like someone wasn't there for you, whether or not they were physically present. It might have happened just once, or over and over.

Maybe your parents emotionally abandoned you, or you lacked their physical presence when you needed it most. Maybe your father or mother actually left. Or maybe your emotional needs were never addressed, or you felt misunderstood and not seen and heard the way you needed to be.

Sometimes, abandonment can take other forms. Maybe you believed you were too sensitive and felt everything too deeply, so you turned your feeling tap off a long time ago. But while that might have enabled your physical or emotional survival at the time, it's now a liability. Don't feel bad that you did it, because so did I. But if you want to have your dream life and that deep inner knowing that truly anything is possible, you're going to need to deal with your abandoned little girl.

Maybe, growing up, you felt like you were too much and your personality was too big. Maybe you were too intense or too quirky. All of these traits are beautiful, but not all families know how to support them.

If yours didn't, then guess what? Your little girl felt abandoned.

But guess who also abandoned you? You!

Holy shit, that was a truthbomb, wasn't it? I know.
Take a minute. Take a few deep breaths. Fully let this in. Now, I don't want you to go into self-blame, 'cos that's a dead-end street. Instead, I want you to access the deep part of yourself that's yearning for you to connect with her...

This deeper part of you is your inner little girl, and she needs you now more than ever. You turned your back on her and abandoned her because you felt abandoned by your parents. It didn't feel safe to keep your heart open. So you slammed the door shut, and that's where your need to stay safe was born.

Now it probably feels tempting to ignore this truth and shove it back in the closet. Stay with me though, gorgeous woman. It's worth figuring this stuff out so you can deal with it once and for all.

I want you to get SUPER-clear on the fact that the problem isn't just being abandoned. Like I said above, the problem is that you abandoned yourself a long time ago. You made a subconscious decision to not allow yourself to be emotional because it wasn't accepted. Or maybe you decided to not allow yourself to be sensitive because it felt too scary, and nobody supported you in believing that sensitivity was safe.
So that abandonment you're feeling is also coming from your betrayal of yourself. It's the result of you abandoning your own light, your own gifts, your own voice and your own expression.
Of COURSE you're scared to let love in! Of COURSE you're scared to commit to another human being. You haven't committed to yourself yet. You've internalized all the messages that the people around you sent about not being OK the way you were, and believed them above your own experience.

Trust me: I know exactly how that goes. Growing up, I was a scared little girl. I used to bite my nails down to the quick. I feared bedtime every single night because my ultra-vivid imagination left me panicking that the boogie man was coming to get me. Then, from the age of about eight onwards, I developed an intense terror of burglars.

I'd obsessively look under the curtains eighteen times before I went to sleep to make myself feel safe and somehow in control. People around me often told me I was too sensitive, so I dimmed my light when my emotional sensitivity was actually my superpower. Maybe it's yours too, but you squashed it down because a parent told you something like:

- "Suck it up! Be strong - there's no point in wasting time crying. That's weak, and in our family, we just get on with it."
- "Men don't like emotional women. If you want a good man, you can't bring your over-reacting and sensitivities into your relationship."
- "No man likes a woman who wears her heart on her sleeve. You have to be mysterious."
- "No one wants to hear about all your feelings. It's self-indulgent and boring, so keep them to yourself."

MY LITTLE GIRL RAN MY LIFE

As I shared with you earlier, my father died instantly when I was eight years old. I had no time to prepare for his loss, and I loved him so much that it broke my heart into a million pieces. I'll never forget the day I found out – and on that day, my little girl subconsciously closed down her heart.

That was it. She closed me down for business. She threw out the key and put a padlock on my heart. From that day forward, love felt absolutely terrifying to me. My little girl thought, "Well, if someone that loved me that much," [and my father DID love me that much,] "and they can still be taken from me, why on earth would I ever even think about letting love in at that level again?" NO WAY!

This was all very subconscious, of course. But that little girl inside me was running my life right up until I was 30 years old. It didn't matter what I did. It didn't matter what healer I saw or what healing modality I tried – whether it was hypnotherapy, NLP, EFT tapping, kinesiology, Reiki, psychics or anything else.

None of it changed the way I related to love, because this little girl was behind the steering wheel of my life. She'd made it her life's work to keep me safe, protect me and keep love away.

Love just set off alarm bells for her... it was a huge red flag that signaled danger!

And beauty, this is what's actually going on at a cellular level for you.

These messages above are what cause you to abandon your little girl.

But the epic news is that it's not too late to get her back. And when you do, she has the keys to the kingdom of everything that you desire.

So let's obliterate the shitty belief you formed in response to those messages once and for all. That belief doesn't belong to you. It's not yours. It's been dimming your light right up until this moment to identify yourself as someone who doesn't need emotions. Emotions are your superpower! It's time to get your feelings on.

Ready? OK, let's lock and load.

YOU'VE BEEN PLAYING SAFE

So can you see that you've built your belief systems around keeping yourself safe? That's been your little girl's full-time job, and she's incredibly loyal. But you've got to get that little girl out from behind the steering wheel. For a start, she can barely see over the dashboard (she's only three or four!) And even more than that, you need to take supreme care of her from this moment on.

To do that, you need to start embodying that higher-self version of yourself: your inner Queen, who knows it's your birthright to let love in. That Queen self knows that love is safe. She knows she can be the chosen one, and that you don't need to fear losing love.

> *The truth is that nothing's guaranteed in this life other than death and taxes.*

One of the things I see a lot with the beautiful women I work with is that they try to approach love while holding back and playing safe. They're out there on the apps. They're dating online. Maybe they're going to singles parties, speed dating, you name it... But they're doing it all with major emotional protection.

If you do this too, it's like you're going out into the world with a suit of armor on. I refer to this as wearing your "love armor". Even if your soulmate were right in front of you, you wouldn't let yourself connect with him. Why? Because your deeper belief is that you've got to keep yourself safe, and it's not OK to let love in.

If this is true for you, you'll notice yourself:

- Continually attracting in emotionally unavailable men who don't bring in their hearts.
- Blaming any problems on timing, convincing yourself it's not the right time or that you're not ready.
- Drinking too much on dates and sabotaging any potential relationships because you don't know who to be and love freaks you out.
- Letting your fears and insecurities make you needy, then going into overdrive to make the relationship work when you feel him pulling away.
- Feeling more invested in keeping your guy happy and adapting to what he wants than you are in honoring yourself.
- Presenting a version of yourself that you think the guy would like, and not knowing who to be when things start to get serious.
- Playing games in your relationships because you don't trust yourself or know how to be in your power.

Doing any of these things puts you out of alignment with yourself. That means dating becomes a complete waste of your time and energy.

I KNOW YOU'RE SCARED, BUT YOU HAVE TO CHOOSE

I'm the first to admit that love is about taking a risk. And by 'risk', I don't mean going after bad boys and ignoring red flags on dates. Instead, I mean risking your heart.

You need to open your heart to someone and keep it open if he doesn't turn out to be your King. I know that can feel mighty uncomfortable, but love isn't created inside your comfort zone. Safe, boring, disconnected relationships are, sure - but not real, heart-connected love. Love ALWAYS happens outside of your comfort zone. It happens when you're willing to be ALL of who you truly are, instead of pretending to be who you think you should be.

If you're just interested in changing your life, you'll do what's comfortable and convenient. If you're committed, you'll do whatever it takes and become a pro at being uncomfortable.

That's the risk I'm talking about. You need to risk being ALL of you, now and forever. You need to risk leading with your heart instead of protecting it. How will your King ever find you if you keep shutting down your heart each time something doesn't work out?

Now, of course, this requires discernment. Your heart is reserved for a very important person - and right now, my darling, that's you. You need to start by holding yourself in high regard and love yourself more and more every day (which is the work, by the way. If you can do that, you'll have your own back, and strengthen your foundation. And when that happens, it won't be hard to keep your heart open and ready for the right man to flow into your life.

I know this feels scary - but it's way riskier to keep protecting yourself and your heart. If you do that, you risk NEVER attracting in the big love you dream of. So it's time to get some perspective on the topic of risk. It's time to create an epic new story for yourself...

- that taking risks is easy for you
- that keeping your heart open and available feels exciting
- that men love and adore the real you
- that you're a rockstar at love
- that keeping your heart safe isn't an option anymore, because it's sabotaging your love from coming in.

Changing this story is about expanding into new possibilities and undiscovered territory with an open heart. This is the place where miracles live. You won't experience this new land - or your big love - if you're more committed to knowing the outcome in advance. That's just your inner control freak (and your little girl) holding on for dear life to keep your heart safe.

There's nothing predictable about love.

There's also nothing safe about love. You have to put yourself on the line.

Do you want to go to your deathbed having stayed safe? Or do you want to go having been loved?

Those are your choices right now. So CHOOSE.

Without a powerful decision, you won't see any change in your life. Period!

I invite you to give up this fear that's holding you hostage: that love isn't safe, that it's scary, that men are shit, that you've been hurt before or that marriage doesn't work anyway. Give up all those beliefs and thoughts and conversations that keep reinforcing that love isn't safe. They all suck royally, and they need to be taken out with the rubbish ASAP.

Incidentally, we're going to throw out a lot of rubbish on this journey together. And I want you to start by visualizing yourself taking out the rubbish that you've been feeding yourself. Burn it out of your life. You can only have one story that guides you, so make sure it's a powerful one.

BEING FAKE WILL GET YOU FAKE RESULTS

Admit it: you aren't walking around as the woman you were born to be. You're not walking around plugged into your glorious deserve-ability or leading with who you truly are. Nor are you sitting in your stunning internal confidence, in the belief that you can genuinely have what you want.

Instead, you show up on dates as this 20% version of yourself.

You show up as the 'fun girl' version of yourself. You know: the version that's great at chatting and dating. You say the right things. You order the right food. You ask the right questions. You certainly don't share too much.

All the while, you're trying so freaking hard to get it right. You're desperate to fit into this version of who you think you should be on these dates. And however hard you try, it never works.

What we've got to address here is that you aren't speaking up with your true voice. You're not bringing in the magical parts of who you actually are. You're not bringing in your inherent humor or quirkiness. Perhaps you're worried to share too much or go too deep, because it hasn't felt safe in the past.

And all these shitty, stifled, held-back ways of being go directly into your Vortex. They stack up on top of each other. Then, together, they build more and more resistance. They take up precious energy in your Vortex that you could use to create with instead. They deplete your Vortex of clarity and aligned intentional focus.

Remember: we attract what we think about and what we give our energy to. If you're holding back your expression, feelings and desires, that will show up in your Vortex. You'll just keep rehashing more of the same, because by holding yourself back on a date, you're shitting in your own Vortex. You're bringing in your belief that you can't get what you want by being all of yourself - so that's exactly what you're creating.

Your Vortex is your precious launchpad of creation, but if you aren't working from a clean launchpad, you'll just keep reproducing mediocre outcomes. You'll keep getting more frustrated and bitter. That's why it's so damn important to shed the shit from your life and to clean up the victimhood ways of being, STAT.

Holding yourself back is like driving with the brakes on - you just don't get anywhere. Then you wonder why this man isn't pursuing you the way that you want to be pursued. That's because, honestly, you're being a fraud. If you only show up with a part of yourself, you won't be satisfied with your dates (or your relationships) EVER. It's also why the dates don't eventuate into a relationship. Or, if they do, you get a year into the relationship and suddenly ask yourself, *"Do I even like this person?"* as you realize you haven't been getting what you needed all this time.

That's when people turn to couple's therapy, and it's all a hot mess.

This happens because, from the get-go, you didn't bring yourself into the relationship. Why? Because you're terrified deep down, not only of love, but also to be who you truly are. The thought of letting someone see the real you is out of bounds. It's off-limits. It's like doing backcountry, Double Black Diamond ski runs. It's like, "Whoa, I could lose my life doing this!"

That's what vulnerability feels like, and it's why you don't bring in who you really are. Which is completely inauthentic, because - believe it or not - men want to see the real you, just like you want to see the real them.

I'll talk about vulnerability more in Chapter 11, because it's something you can't cut corners with. It requires you to dive deep into sharing who you really are with no coping mechanisms, masks or justifications. But take it from me - vulnerability is well worth it, because everything becomes possible when you're willing to be vulnerable.

So no more being stingy and selective with your heart. Open it and keep it open if you want to live a deeply fulfilling, lit-up life.

YOU'LL ONLY GET WHAT YOU WANT
WHEN YOU'RE ALL OF WHO YOU ARE

When Susie came to me, she was downright perplexed about why she couldn't get love to work for her. She was a beautiful, blonde, British woman who quite frankly could be a top model AND she had such a divine energy. But she'd already given up on love after a string of failed relationships, and she was talking to me about her Plan B (more on Plan Bs later!) of having a baby on her own.

Not only did Susie no longer trust men, but she was massively in her masculine energy. That meant she was only bringing 20% at most of who she was into relationships. So men would start off keen as mustard with her, and then lose interest just as fast.

Once Susie started doing my deep process, she came home to who she truly was at a soul level. She started to really like what she saw. She realized that up, until that moment, she'd been hiding her true self because she was so scared of more rejections.

And then, once she opened her heart and got to love the real Susie, she couldn't contain it. Her heart started to fill up with all of her own divine love and acceptance. She felt safe – and even excited – to be vulnerable in all areas of her life.

This was such a huge shift for her: she managed to completely change her life on every level. For example, she quit her job as a vet and is now giving 100% of her focus and energy to creating her own yoga business. That was something she'd always wanted to do, but had been too scared to try.

More than that though, Susie's now loved up with her soulmate... and she's still in awe of the courage she found within herself to do

> *this deep work. She and her man are now talking about starting a family, and she's living in the land of miracles and love. So many other opportunities are coming her way too because she's open to receiving them.*
>
> *That's what living in your feminine energy and vulnerability looks like: there's flow, ease, trust, grace, a shitload of heart energy AND no Plan B. Can you feel that?*

Let me tell you something: Susie's not the only one who had that fear. That was me too.

I thought I was all that. Before each date, I'd go and have my hair blow-dried. I'd get a new dress. I'd wear new earrings. I'd have a cheeky glass of champagne. Then I'd show up as this version of who I thought I needed to be for the man to like me. And the worst part is that I didn't even check in to figure out, *"Do I actually like you?"*

My MO was to make sure that the guy liked me. It came from a place of lack - a place of not-enough-ness, of overcompensating, of wanting to be liked and 'get it right'. Now that makes me want to throw up in my lap, because it's so fucking inauthentic. And yet that's how I used to roll for years until I woke up and got sick of not getting what I wanted in love and life.
I went out on these dates and left Lucy at the door every single time. I may as well have called myself Sonya. I could have told my dates, "Hi, I'm Sonya, nice to meet you. Don't expect Lucy. She's checked out."

On the plus side, looking at it this way is very powerful, because you can see that there's nothing confusing about the picture at all. It's not that love doesn't work for you. It's that you've been running from love and yourself your entire life, because keeping yourself safe has been more important. It's been more important to come across looking good than to be who you truly are.

Of course, when you do this, you put a discordant energy into your Vortex. Then you end up attracting in the wrong men because you're out of alignment with who you really are. Everyone loses when you pretend.

And so many amazing women who come to me have given up on love because it's draining them. It's exhausting. It's not fun. It's not intimate. Keeping up this charade steals all your good energy and robs you of the future you deserve with your divine man in it. So sister, it is past time to give that shit up!

RESCUING IS A BAD HABIT THAT'S KEEPING YOU OUT OF ALIGNMENT

One of the most common paradigms I see in my clients is rescuing. That's where you go into a relationship to try to help or fix someone. And let me tell you, that was me. It suited me to attract in men who were very handsome on the exterior. They were sexy as fuck, and had it ALL going on. But when I look back, I realize that all these guys had one thing in common - they were non-committing Peter Pans.

Then again, so was I.

So of course, this just kept happening. It was how I was hardwired - all because, many years ago, I'd subconsciously told myself the shitty story that I wasn't soulmate material. Love was so terrifying to me that I just kept playing this role like an actor. I felt like I was a doctor with a waiting room of men who'd come to me so I could rescue and fix them.

Why did I do this for so long? Because it was much easier to focus on helping someone else than it was to actually let myself be loved and have the spotlight on me. If I was in the spotlight, heaven forbid, I'd be vulnerable. Someone would see who I really was, with all my flaws and fears.
So instead, I subconsciously attracted in men who were a little bit lost, or who had mother issues or who were off-purpose. And for me, it was almost like a little project where I got to put all my focus

into trying to prop them up instead of getting my own needs met. And that, of course, is not a foundation that you want to start any relationship from.

If you take a closer look at your own track record, I bet you anything you'll see you're doing this in your life too. Not just with men, either. Maybe you're doing it in friendships, family relationships and even at work. It's showing up everywhere, all over your life.

Because how we show up in one area of life is how we show up in every area of life.

Usually, this pattern goes back to your childhood where you had to be someone else's caretaker. Maybe you had an alcoholic mother or a parent with clinical depression or you were the eldest sibling. Maybe your mother was grieving, maybe she didn't have her shit together, or maybe she'd just completely checked out.

However it showed up in your life, you had to step up and put your own needs aside. The exact form doesn't matter: as children, we take stuff on without thinking about it. We're adaptable and good at surviving. That's great - it got you here. But it's NOT serving you now. It's time to break up with this rescuing role and start putting yourself first.

When you're being the rescuer, you go into over-giving and overcompensating because you don't have boundaries (and we've talked about how important those are already). Essentially, you turn into a doormat. You're busy trying to fill up your love tank by making someone else feel better. You lose your own identity because you don't value who you are.

It's toxic, and - as you know - it doesn't feel good.

The worst part about being a rescuer is that the guy inevitably ends up leaving you. Once he starts to get his love tank filled up, he just moves on to the next woman, and then goes and marries her. I definitely rescued many men who did that. And there's nothing more frustrating and upsetting than when you do your best work to get someone else ready, and then they don't choose you. They leave you because your relationship is imbalanced, and you're coming to it from your masculine. And at your core, you're coming from a need for major protection, lack and fear of letting love in.

Can you see that now?

Being a rescuer doesn't feel powerful. It doesn't lead to anything good. You can't have a soulmate relationship while you're living out of the rescuing paradigm. You need to be your own soulmate first, which is terrifying if you've never done it before!

Are you nodding your head and saying, "This is me, Lucy. I'm the rescuer, but I'm scared to put my own needs first and make them a priority"? If so, then right now, I'm inviting you to break up with ever uttering those words again.

You are not here to fix other people.

You are not here to heal other people.

You are not here to rescue anyone.

You ARE here to step into all the glory of who you were born to be. You're here to take up space in the world and allow yourself to be supported. The only way that will happen is by you making it your priority to love, value and treasure yourself every single day. You get to create the life you want and choose to let love in through your Vortex. And you can do this even when that feels scary.

I hope you're crystal clear about the significance of putting your own needs and juicy desires first.

Because again, until it's about you,
it's never going to be about you.

And until you invest in yourself, no one's going to invest in you. It all starts with you being your own priority - no 'if's or 'but's.

In the next chapter, we'll talk about how damaging it is for you to pretend to be 'fine', because along with the fear of actually letting love in, it's one of the big stumbling blocks to attracting your soulmate.

THE GOLD NUGGETS

Beautiful woman, we've covered some gold together in the last few pages. Here's a quick recap of the 24-karat nuggets to take away with you and treasure as you head into the next chapter:

• The reason your soulmate hasn't shown up yet is that your little girl is in the driver's seat, and she decided long ago that love wasn't safe.

• Because of that, she's terrified to let love in now.

• Rescuing men (or anyone else) doesn't serve you - it just drains you and creates inauthentic connections.

• To take control of your life back, you need to take charge and step into your Queen self - you're here to be ALL of yourself.

• The future is yours to claim, so get excited about speaking your new story into existence.

GIFT WORK

Over to you, superstar! Go through the exercises that follow to get to know your little girl, and dig into what scares you so much about letting love in.

First up, it's time to meditate! Go to the book bonuses page at _www. soultosoulglobal.com/book-bonuses_ and listen to the meditation on how to connect with and heal your little girl. Commit to doing this meditation every day to really give your little girl a chance to express herself, and allow yourself to heal her.

Then, once you've connected to your little girl, journal your answers to the following questions:

- How old is your little girl? Note that there's probably more than one little girl active in you at any time. My most dominant one is eight, but I have a three-year-old, a 16-year-old, and a 21-year-old too.
- Ask each of them what they need.
- What emotions come up when you do this?

Let each little girl know you will love and support her from this moment on.

Next, close your eyes and imagine holding each little girl in your arms, one at a time. Let her know you love her and wait until you feel it before you finish making the connection with her. Don't be disheartened - this connection can take time to build, so keep checking in with her every day.

Finally, journal your answers to these questions:

- What is the energy around your connection?
- What does it make you feel? Describe everything!
- Observe each little girl. What is she showing you? What is she saying to you?

CHAPTER EIGHT

I'm fine.

NO REALLY, I AM.

"It's time to get real with yourself and the world."

I know I talked about your inner little girl a lot in the last chapter, but she's going to crop up again and again. That's because - as we discussed - up till now, SHE's been running your life from behind the scenes. She's been doing everything in her power to make sure love doesn't work out for you.

So if you don't feel lit and in flow, it's because you're stuck in being 'fine'. And - like I said earlier - that's a dead-end street where nothing good ever happens.

Stop hiding behind feeling 'fine'. Instead, start feeling what's TRULY there for you. Drop into those precious emotions and let yourself marinate in them. Once you're willing to do that, beauty, you can create anything you want.

YOU'RE LIVING A LIE

I'd like to bring your attention to two of the most overused words on the planet: I'm fine.

"No, really. I'm fine. I'm good." How often have you asked someone how they are, and heard them reply, "I'm fine. Everything's good." And when you hear it, how often do you know that the truth is the complete opposite?

It happens all the time, right?

This is honestly such a dangerous way to live, my darling. Back before my big AHA moment, I even had myself fooled. I was one of those people who put on a public persona that 'everything was fine'. I even convinced myself I was OK.

That's the scariest part. I pretended and kept showing that sunny version of myself to the outside world for so damn long because I didn't want to be a burden to anyone. I didn't feel worthy enough to show anyone just how UN-FINE I was. Nor could I let myself connect with the truth of how unhappy I actually was.

It very quickly brings so many of my clients to their knees when they fully get the magnitude of the lie that they've been living. They've been operating out of this identity for so long that, just like I did, they've tricked themselves into believing they're fine. They've begun to accept that this is just the way life is. It's a whole setup of smoke and mirrors, where they genuinely believe, *"It's just going to happen. I'm really, really close to it now. So I'm good."*

That's a massive trap.

STOP HIDING BEHIND THE BS THAT 'ONE' BIT OF YOUR LIFE ISN'T WORKING

Piper, a gorgeous Australian woman, was on the phone with me just recently. She had a beautiful, sunny energy... and I know for a fact that if I was living in Australia, we'd totally hang out. But during our call, I could hear so much coping going on that I couldn't connect with the real Piper.

I asked her, "Could you just take off your mask for a minute?" I wanted her to show me who she really was.

Initially, she had no idea what that meant. She replied, "No,

EIGHT | I'm fine. **NO REALLY, I AM.**

this IS the real me. Honestly. I'm good. I meditate. I have good friends. I go out all the time. I go on cool trips. I've got a great life. Sure, there's just this one part of my life that's not working, but everything else is perfect."

Like I've said before, I'm a straight shooter, so I wasn't going to let her get away with BS-ing herself like that. I asked why, exactly, we were on the call if everything was so great. And then I told her, woman to woman, that she was so disconnected from herself that I couldn't even reach her. I knew it would hit her like a ton of bricks, but that was good because waking people up is exactly what I'm here to do.

Then I went on, "Piper, I wish someone had woken me up ten years ago the way I'm waking you up now. I know it's not comfortable, but you need to get that your 'I'm fine!' is keeping you separated from the outside world. It's keeping you separated from even your closest friends! And the truth is that you feel lonely and dead inside, am I right?"

For a moment, there was silence as Piper just absorbed what I'd said. Then she replied, "Holy shit, there's SO much truth in that, Lucy. A huge part of me feels numb. I guess I do feel dead!" She hadn't ever admitted it to herself, but my words created a visceral reaction within her. It was like I'd just pulled the rug from under her and wiped the fake smile off her face.

As she reflected on her reaction, she realized she was terrified to let anyone in. She wasn't sure she even could. I could hear the tears in her voice when she admitted, "I don't even know

who the real Piper IS!" and asked me if I could help.
I told her I did this kind of thing all the time, but that it would
take full-blown commitment from her. She knew she couldn't
go on the way she had been though, so she said, "I understand.
Let's do this, Lucy!"

Like most of my clients, Piper went on to change her entire
life. She was blown away at how quickly she started to feel
good... like incredibly good. She began to genuinely love
herself. Friends started asking her who the new man was, even
though she didn't have one yet! She was like a little girl with
a big secret, and she couldn't stop smiling.

On top of that, she got a pay rise and a promotion without even
asking for it. That wasn't a coincidence: it happened because
she'd shifted out of the fake, trying-to-please-everyone
energy and into her enough-ness and receiving energy.

Now she feels unstoppable, and has no shadow of a doubt that
her 'soulie' will be coming in soon.

IT'S NOT THE MAN THAT'S MISSING, IT'S YOU

Being 'fine' is a common symptom of doing self-development intellectually instead of feeling it and doing the deeper work, which I spoke about in Chapter 5. Just like Piper, women say to me all the time, "I meditate. I go for daily walks. I've got good friends. I've got all this stuff going on. The only tiny little piece that's missing is the man."

*I've got news for you: it's NOT
the man who's missing.*

This is the illusion I want to smash right now. It's not the man. We should never, ever want a man to complete us, because that means we're incomplete to begin with. We can absolutely desire to have a relationship. Hellz to the yes. Why wouldn't we? That's why you're reading this book, right?

At the same time, I want you to check in with yourself. If you're saying, "I've got everything. It's great. I'm just missing a guy," that's a giant red flag. It's showing you how out of alignment with yourself you are.

What's missing from this whole equation isn't a man. Instead, it's a strong, intimate relationship with yourself.

Constantly repeating, "I'm fine," is just a coping mechanism. And it's one that's keeping you from getting support. More importantly, it's keeping you from connecting with your truth.
That truth is confronting. It's uncomfortable. I remember back when I first let my truth hit me. It was like a fricking A380 airplane landing in my living room. It felt insanely huge, and it didn't fit with everything I'd been telling myself.

I realized that, holy shit, I'd been in major fucking denial. The truth was that I was numb, but I'd been getting around it, thinking I was being really authentic. I thought I was so self-expressed. I knew that I was technically a good catch. I kept telling myself all that, but deep down... I didn't believe it at all.

Instead, I'd bought into the idea that everything was fine. I insisted that if I just kept doing my affirmations, a man would come into my life. But then, as I mentioned, I'd numb myself during weekends with my girlfriends over a few bottles of champers. (I mean, yes, it was bloody fabulous champagne. But
I only drank it to suppress all my unfulfilled desires that, year after year, didn't come to fruition. I drank it to numb myself and avoid facing my truth or feeling my deep, underlying pain.)

And sister, until you're willing to actually face yourself and deal with the truth of just how far away you are from your goal, you'll keep living in the world of pretending too. You'll keep living in denial, and in coping, and it's never going to get you what you want.

BEING FINE IS COSTING YOU EVERYTHING

One of my rockstar clients, Coco, cried a river in our first 48 hours of working together, after fully getting the magnitude of this conversation. She was just devastated. She told me, "Lucy, I was even trying to avoid things on our breakthrough call because I was still trying to keep it all together. I was still trying to convince myself that I didn't need this support."

She admitted to me afterward that she'd tried to withhold as much as she could because she wanted to show me that she was totally fine. And that was even though her heart told her that she wanted to work with me, so she knew on some level that things WEREN'T 'fine'.

But on the call, she'd felt this deep, deep sensation coming up inside of her that she wasn't expecting. She'd tried to turn a blind eye to it, but thankfully, it had won. It was something bigger than herself – the admission, for the first time that, "You know what? I'm not fine, and something needs to change NOW!"

Coco went on to do phenomenal work with me. Her big, beautiful heart opened, and her light turned on. And then, once she got the taste of who she actually was and her real power, she said she felt like she'd won the lottery. She vowed

> *to never turn her back on herself again.*
>
> *Since that moment, she's up-leveled her business massively, because she now trusts herself and knows her full capability. And not only that, but she's also having a ball attracting and dating a completely different caliber of men.*

I know from my own journey how numb I was. It's not until you have the courage to let yourself feel - and I mean truly feel - your emotions that you'll be able to have a soulmate relationship.

Remember: you have to feel it to heal it.

To attract your soulmate, it's super-important to not compartmentalize your feelings. You simply can't walk around with everything 'handled'.

BEING 'FINE' IS TOXIC AF!

In order to thrive as a woman in the world, you have to reconnect to those deep, buried feelings within, because they show you where you are. Staying disconnected is basically like walking around as a cardboard cutout version of yourself.

Not only that, but sadness, grief, resentment and anger can turn toxic if you leave them unfelt and undealt with. As we've talked about before, when you feel them, you can transmute them into gold. But when you leave them buried, they can turn into dis-ease (as the name clearly states, that means you're causing less ease in your body)! Switching the emotional tap off and going to the land of 'I'm fine' is detrimental to your health. It's totally toxic.

So turning a blind eye and refusing to deal with your emotions will cause you more harm than feeling them ever would. You know how

they put those little stickers on cigarette packets?
We should have some for ourselves too. We should put stickers on our human bodies that say, "If you're not feeling right now, you are causing great harm." That's how important feeling is. Continuing to stuff down your emotions and your precious truth is impacting your health!

Remember that the reason you stuff your feelings down under a blanket of 'I'm fine' or eat / drink / drug them away, is because your inner little girl doesn't feel safe to express herself. So when women start getting to work in my *Soul to Soul* program, it's often the first time they allow themselves to feel. That can be overwhelming initially, but it's also life-changing, and it gets easier the more they do it. They very quickly tap into their essence and full ability to feel again. It's like watching a wilting flower spring back to life, and it's so fucking powerful and magical to witness.

So, as you're reading this, you might feel some emotions coming up. You may not know what to do with them, but you know there's something about this that resonates with you. If so, I want you to know that I see you, darling. Give yourself over to these feelings. You don't have to label them. You don't need to think about them, or break them down, or analyze and compartmentalize them. Just let them come up.

Good is the enemy of great.

You can't afford to buy into society's story anymore. You can't indulge in avoidance and pushing things down the way you've done in the past. How do you know when you're doing that? Things to watch for - impulses you'll have - that can signal a coverup and a stuff-down might include:

- The urge to just slap a smile on.
- Doing your affirmations on autopilot.
- Thinking that yoga is enough.
- Reaching for the glass(es) of wine to drown out that feeling.
- The desire to run away, pretend it's not happening, dance to a

cool song or just flat-out pretend that you're happy.

I did that for years. I could literally cry when I think of how much time I wasted. It would have been so much quicker and more effective to just feel what I was feeling... but that didn't even occur as an option for me.

Back then, that didn't feel safe for me at all.

DON'T DO YOUR FEELINGS, FEEL THEM

Feeling your feelings can sound pretty simple. But, like all simple stuff, it can feel pretty damn challenging to do - at least until you've done it.

To start, all you need to do is give over to this deeper part of yourself. Let your feelings come up. But once you begin, be ready. There's a lifetime of stuffed-down feelings - feelings upon feelings upon feelings, resentment upon resentment upon resentment - that need to be felt. There are needs upon needs upon needs that weren't met.

And they'll ALL start to come to the surface. So you need to be ready to deal with them, beautiful! It's time to put your superhero cape on and strap into your courage. You can so do this.

Don't be surprised, once you start allowing yourself to connect with them, if you find a *shitload* of feelings there. It'll probably feel a little (maybe a lot) overwhelming. You might find yourself wondering why there's such a HUGE volume of crap you need to deal with. Maybe you'll start thinking it means there's something wrong with you - that you're broken in some way.

If so, beautiful woman, I want to remind you that we're ALL like this. Every single one of us. We all have this little girl inside of us who feels like we ignored and abandoned her all those years ago. Remember that, no matter how great your childhood looked on the surface, you still had 'stuff' you didn't have the skills or experience to process. You still pushed shit down and locked it away inside.

Then, as you grew up, that little girl within you felt it every time she was rejected or silenced or told things like:

- "Don't have that dream. It's too big."
- "In our family, we don't do that!"
  (Whatever 'that' might be. For me, it was when I crowdfunded a show in New York and my mum said, "Lucy, we don't crowdfund. If you need the money, I'll help you!" I went ahead and crowdfunded anyway, which required enormous vulnerability from me. And guess what? People were so excited to be able to be part of my one-woman show!)
- "Stop being so emotional. Wipe your tears and get on with it. You have to be strong to survive in this world."
- "Why do you need to earn so much money? It won't make you happy. In our family, we're humble. You just need enough, so stop with this whole needing to be successful thing."
- "You need to be more accommodating with men. Stop having such high standards. You just need a nice man who'll treat you well. You're wrapped up in a fairytale that doesn't exist."

Right now, I'm giving you an opportunity to say, "Enough is enough," to all the crap that silenced your little girl. There are plenty of Hallmark cards out there telling you to, 'just be happy' and that 'everything's great'. Well, everything's NOT fucking great. If you're just 'good' or 'fine', that's preventing you from living an incredible, lit-up, thriving life.

'Fine' is the enemy of fucking fantastic.

I know that the concept of finally letting these feelings come up probably scares the pants off you. It certainly did for me. It felt like opening Pandora's box. So maybe you're thinking that if you open this up, you're not sure what will happen. Maybe you'll cry for a month straight. Well, so what if you do? If that's what you need to do to get yourself feeling and connected to your heart again, you'll just have to cry for a month.

One of my rockstar clients had never cried before she worked with me. Then, during my eight-week program, she cried for six of them and asked me if it would ever stop. I reassured her that yes, it would, but reminded her that she'd opened the floodgates of over 30 years of repressed tears and emotions.

Then I invited her to look at it differently, and to instead celebrate the tears and the massive release that was taking place. She was releasing SO many toxins and so much stagnant energy from her body.

Plus, when you actually give yourself permission to release what needs to come out, you put yourself on a very quick trajectory to healing. And trust me: you're going to feel SO much lighter. It'll be like a huge weight has lifted off your shoulders.

But crying is far from the only reaction you might have. You might also discover that, underneath the tears, there's a pool of white-hot, burning RAGE bubbling and boiling away inside you too. And if so, then WOOHOOO! A-fucking-men, sister. Celebrate that rage. Nurture it. Let yourself bathe in it. Because underneath that rage is where your power is.

In fact, one of the exercises that women who work with me love the most - my Rage Pages - is designed to help you access and express that built-up rage. Writing Rage Pages involves blocking out time to sit down with your pen and paper, and writing out everything you've been burying and not expressing for years. It's about allowing yourself to feel at your deepest heart level: all the anger, all the fury, everything you've shoved down deep where you don't have to acknowledge it. For more about how to work with Rage Pages, see the Gift work section at the end of this chapter.

Keeping up the 'I'm fine' façade is absolute bullshit. I'm telling you now, beauty, you CANNOT tolerate continually showing up in this false positivity, this false optimism. You CANNOT keep slapping a smile on everything to prove to the world that you're fine when deep down, there's nothing fine about your life or how you actually feel.

BEHIND 'I'M FINE', YOUR FUTURE'S ON THE LINE

When I admitted how UN-FINE 'I'm fine' was, I realized that my whole future was riding on it. My fertility was starting to get seriously freaking real. On top of that — like I've said before — I was living in New York City, where everyone talks about how tough love is over twelve mimosas… but they're still 'fine'!

Watching my dream slipping through my fingers was starting to feel incredibly confronting, so I said to myself, "Lucy, you're not fine at all. This isn't just going to happen on its own. What you're doing right now isn't working. So, you'd better get out there and make this your fucking priority, because this ain't fixing itself. Otherwise, you'll turn 40 single and alone, and miss the opportunity to ever have children."

For me personally, that outcome was like a death sentence. It wasn't something that I was willing to allow. And THANK GOD I recognized that, or I wouldn't be speaking to you from the place I'm in now, with an amazing soulmate and a beautiful daughter.

So please, divine woman, let this conversation really affect you. Let it sink in. If tears are coming up, let them roll. If you feel a pit in your stomach, or any other uncomfortable sensations, celebrate that. I'll be celebrating it with you because you're doing the work!

YOU CAN DO THIS

I want to leave you with just one message in this chapter. Are you telling yourself that you'll meet someone - that everything's fine and it'll just all work out? Are your friends telling you, "Don't worry sweetie, you'll be fine. Next year is your year, and it's the Chinese Year of the Dog (or whatever it might be)"?

We can hang on to so many things like our star signs, or where the moon is placed, and use them to trick ourselves into believing that everything is fine. So many women tell me, "Lucy, I'm so close. I know I'm so close. I know my man is just about to come in."

If this is you, I want you to know that I was in that story too. When I added up how long I'd been saying that to myself, it came to ten frigging years. TEN years until I suddenly woke up at 36 and went, *"Holy fucking shit! I'm not fine, and this is still not happening. Nothing I've done has been effective."*

That's a bloody uncomfortable place to be, so I want to acknowledge you for even continuing to read the words in front of you. That shows that you're a woman who's on her way to changing her life.

Yes, of course, it'll feel uncomfortable. Your emotional tap has been turned off for many, many years now. So of course it's collected a lot of cobwebs. Of course the water's a little rusty. Of course crying feels scary. Of course feeling anything is scary.

Dealing with all the shit feels daunting. I get it. But it's also vital if you want to finally step into being the incredible woman that you are. You deserve love. And better yet, you'll have it if you choose a much better story than the one you've been telling.

You're NOT 'fine' right now... but you will be!

THE GOLD NUGGETS

Beautiful woman, we've covered some gold together in the last few pages. Here's a quick recap of the 24-karat nuggets to take away with you and treasure as you head into the next chapter:

- If your life is 'fine' except for one thing, you're NOT fine - and if that thing is 'not having a soulmate', you're putting your power outside of yourself.

- Being 'fine' is a way of shutting off, hiding from the truth and staying in a holding pattern that only leads you deeper and deeper into Numb City.

- 'Fine' is also the enemy of 'fucking fantastic', and to get past it, you need to let yourself feel - and deal with - whatever's really there for you.

- One great technique for accessing and expressing any rage you uncover is my Rage Pages exercise.

- If you also need to crank up the music and then cry or rage out loud, that's totally OK - it's powerful, even if it feels terrifying.

GIFT WORK

Over to you, superstar! It's time to dig deep and release the hurt
that you've tucked away in the closet. Let's stop it derailing every
relationship you start or get close to starting.

It's time to get to know Rage Pages. I recommend doing these at night.
If you live with flatmates or family, let them know you'll be cranking up
some music because there's stuff you've got to take care of. If they're
out or you live alone, even better. Be respectful but unapologetic.

To do this exercise, you need to focus on your little girl. Get a notebook
or journal, then set the scene. Put on some lovely, soft music and light
a candle. Put your hands over your heart space, and drop into your
memories of childhood. You can't do this wrong, darling woman.

Just allow the feeling and memories to surface. Allow yourself to focus
on times when your needs weren't met, or where you weren't seen or
validated. Just allow whatever comes to your mind, and feel it. Trust the
images that come to you.

Then, once you start to feel the sensations in your body, as you're
beginning to get triggered, get your pen and start writing! Use
the prompts below to write without censoring yourself, so you can
reconnect with your truth on a deep level:

- What experience / trauma do you need to feel and release to
  successfully move forward?
- Which parent are you trying to please? Don't protect them - allow
  the truth to come up. They won't ever see this!
- Which parent are you trying to prove your worth to or feeling let
  down by?

  (And for my women who had a 'fantastic childhood', this
  absolutely applies to you. It's detective work that will reveal why
  you're struggling to attract your King, so make sure you commit
  to connecting with your little girl so she can share her truth with
  you.)
- Which parent treated you badly or spoiled you? Write down how
  they treated you, whether it was good, bad or indifferent. What

did you want from them?

And now that you know exactly where your little girl's coming from, here are some further questions to take you deeper. They'll help you to see exactly what you've stuffed down under the surface of 'I'm fine':

- Where have you sold out on yourself in relationships and in your dreams?
- What event, trauma or experience have you been blocking or numbing that's still sucking your life-force energy?

   (And if you're reluctant to connect with this, that's exactly why it's so important. I'm holding a huge space for you, so please surrender to your truth and let it all come up. You're so courageous for doing this, and I bow down to you in this moment!)

Then simply allow everything to come up. Cry and express yourself however you need to in order to truly move through it. Let it get messy and real as FUCK!

Have deep reverence for yourself for accessing these uncomfortable parts of you. I'm so proud of you! And then, once you've had this huge release, crank up some fun tunes to create some good energy again and shake it all off!

CHAPTER NINE

Independence and
BODYGUARDS

*"The Universe can only bring us
who we are for ourselves."*

So many women proudly describe themselves as 'independent' and wear the term as a badge of honor. That independence is a super-masculine identity that means they don't need support... but underneath it lies the terror of love that we talked about in Chapter 8. Then they back up their independence with a squad of internal bodyguards to keep them even safer.

Together, their independence and bodyguards create a false sense of security... and also keep them alone and very single. What they need to focus on instead is healthy interdependence in a soulmate relationship - one where both partners stand on their own two feet AND support each other powerfully and spaciously.

"BUT BEING INDEPENDENT IS WHO I AM!"

This could be the shortest chapter in the book, because seriously, beauty, all you need to know is in the next two paragraphs.

I hear it so often. "Lucy, I want to keep my independence in a soulmate relationship. How do I do that?"

Here's the quick answer: NOT possible.

I know. You need to pick yourself up off the floor. Hearing that goes against everything you've built up for yourself. It goes against how you see yourself and how you show up in the world.
But you can't hold onto your independence when you're in a soulmate

relationship. The two concepts are like oil and water. They just don't mix. And yet, I'm staggered by the fact that around 99% of the women who come to me keep clinging to their independence. They'll do anything to hold onto their strong, independent identities because they don't want to lose their power.

And it feels fucking TERRIFYING to even consider letting go of it. I'm so excited to get to crack this conversation open. Because your desire to cling to your independence is part of what's keeping you single right now. You've filled your Vortex with independence, and look where it's gotten you! You're leading from your masculine with a checklist, instead of sitting in your divine feminine and being fully open and ready to receive from your heart.

Dictionary.com defines independence as *"freedom from control, influence, support, aid, or the like, of others"*. So when you're independent, you bring all of that 'freedom' into your Vortex.

Look, I used to identify with being independent too. I wanted to keep my freedom. But when I finally got with the program, I flipped this story on its head. My new story included having the most epic soulmate relationship ever with a man who got me. And in our relationship, I felt freedom and acceptance on all levels. So guess what? I'm now married to that guy, and I still feel as free as I did when I was single - except that now I get to share my life with someone amazing... my King!

The very word 'independence' sends a message to the Universe of 'I've got this'. It says, 'I can do this on my own, independent of anyone else's support.' But the irony is, divine one, that deep down, your inner little girl is starving for support and love and intimacy. And you cannot possibly invite in ANY of those things when you've got this armor - this persona and identity - of 'I've got this'.

Insisting on our independence keeps
us from receiving.

NINE | Independence and BODYGUARDS

I INHERITED INDEPENDENCE

Independence is just a construct. It's a buzzword that we modern women have inherited - me just as much as everyone else. I grew up with an incredible mother who was the definition of independent. Remember how my father died when I was eight? Well, for whatever reason, we had to go to school the next day, which sent the message to me that 'I had to be fine'.

It was powerful to see Mum holding the fort like that. She was a pillar of grounded strength, and I'm so deeply grateful for it. But going back to school without taking a moment to digest what had happened was premature. Our feelings about Dad's death were so intense that I think it scared Mum to have us stop to feel them.

I then inherited her strong identity, which definitely didn't serve me once I decided I wanted to attract my soulmate. And clinging to your independent identity isn't serving you either. It completely conflicts with your desire to let love in and be vulnerable in your true divine essence. As we'll talk about in Chapter 11, vulnerability takes courage. It requires letting go of the known to step boldly into the unknown where miracles and possibilities can unfold.

So let's dive a little bit deeper and uncover where your independence originated. Each woman is different, but at the heart of it, we all start to embody 'I've got this' because we didn't feel loved in the way we needed to be as little girls. We weren't getting supported in the ways that we needed.

Now, I firmly believe that all (or at least most) parents do the absolute best they can. But really, that's irrelevant to your little girl. She picks up things at a very young age. So if your father wasn't present - maybe he was busy working or insecure or emotionally withholding or had a bad relationship with your mother or died - your little girl took on that role. Then you stepped up and effectively became 'the father of the family'.

Or perhaps your mum was super-busy with your siblings, and you were the eldest. So you took on a role of responsibility, and never actually got to be a little girl. You didn't get to play or have fun - instead, you learned early on that YOU had to be the responsible one. To avoid being a burden to your mum, you had to be resilient and on top of things. You knew that if you didn't do it, nobody else would.

Or maybe you were the youngest or the middle child, and you took on some other role. Maybe you were over-mothered or never felt like you were important. Regardless of what your circumstances may have been, the result was that you didn't feel like the priority - EVER. And you still don't.

Fully take that in, because THAT's what's showing up in your relationships now. It's happening because you don't know how to let someone else take care of you and support you the way that you need. On top of that, you're not taking care of yourself or even taking the time to ask yourself what you need. And it's all because you never made yourself your own priority.

The great news is that this gets to change right here and now. You can change your internal narrative with just the desire to do so, and the powerful choice to make it about you from here on in. You can change it by putting yourself first with yourself, so that you can then do the same in relationships. Putting yourself first isn't selfish. It's MANDATORY if you want to experience an incredible, healthy, soul-connected relationship.

In addition to what we all learned as little girls, there's also a global message that we need to be strong, independent women. There's this energy of 'I'm going to make things happen - I am woman, hear me roar!' just about everywhere you go.
Now, while I'm ecstatic about women taking up more space in the world, a lot of that energy is extremely masculine. It comes from bravado and proving energy. And once again, it's because, from a very young age, we've shut down our ability to receive.

As women, our truest superpower is in our 'being' energy. It's when we're in our divine feminine, and we can let people see who we truly are. Make no mistake: we still get shit done. We still have plans and dreams. We still have to work to transform them into reality - but we do it from a completely different place. Our divine feminine looks like allowing, trusting and taking inspired action from our hearts, instead of pushing, grinding and 'making it happen' without trust.

Being in that masculine 'I'm OK!' energy is a lot like the 'I'm fine' energy we talked about in the previous chapter. It's keeping you from letting love in, because - if you're honest - it's much easier to be busy than to let yourself be still and feel.

'I've got this!' is keeping you
single and alone.

Take a deep breath, close your eyes and connect with when and how your own 'I've got this' originated.

Did you grow up with a mother or father who told you they wanted you to be independent? Or perhaps you picked up the idea that it was the right thing to do along the way from girlfriends or at university or from mentors?

LETTING GO OF THE NEED TO ACHIEVE

Melissa was an incredible Ivy League graduate, and one of the brightest women I'd ever met. She was seriously driven, but she'd been living her whole life from a masculine energy of 'Do more! Work hard! Achieve, achieve, achieve!'

She said, "Hellz, yes!" to doing the deep work she needed to do, even though she had no idea what that really meant. In her gut, she felt that it was what she needed; and although she was scared, she knew something massive needed to shift.

Melissa had just come out of a relationship where she once

---

again hadn't been the priority, and she was devastated to have wasted yet more time on the wrong guy. She was also suffering from major overachiever-itis. And — surprise, surprise — once we started working together, she discovered that she was showing up in love the same way she was with her academic achievements. It was all 'do, do, do, try harder, be more!'

She knew this wasn't sustainable, and it wasn't getting her what she wanted in love and life. She felt unhappy and had started to question herself. She often wondered, "What's wrong with me? Why can't I figure this out?" And then one day, when she hit the halfway mark of working with me, she took a huge breath, exhaled and said, "OMG, I get it now, Lucy! I was totally in my own way and my heart was closed!"

Melissa realized she'd been trying to do all the work in her head. She'd been seeking external validation and acceptance. She'd gotten her degree to please her dad, and had abandoned the woman she truly was without that degree. She'd needed those achievements and accolades, and had totally lost touch with who she was before them.

It was incredible to witness the moment she surrendered, let go and just let the tears roll. She could finally connect with the essence of who she was and love herself deeply. She also finally acknowledged that she was enough because she was enough — and her 'enough-ness' had nothing to do with her achievements. This was a huge turning point in her life, and she could suddenly feel all her deep resentments and anger, and transmute them into power.

From there, Melissa went on to attract men who DID show

up for her. She stopped people-pleasing, and started valuing herself at a soul level. That meant she could show up with certainty about who she was in the world, instead of constantly seeking other people's approval.

Her heart is now peaceful, and she knows she's worthy of everything she desires. She no longer leads with her degree or academic achievements, but with her heart and who she is instead. And yet, despite her no longer focusing on those external things, she's being offered incredible career opportunities. Not only that, but she's also in hot demand with men who want to treat her like the Queen that she is.

She isn't ready to settle down just yet, but she says her dating life is 'like night and day' compared to what it was. And, of course, she's loving feeling like the priority in every part of her life.

I can tell you with certainty that, yes, there are plenty of independent women in relationships. But there's no real intimacy going on inside those relationships. That's because being independent keeps you from true heart connection. Those independent women may live together with someone. They may be married and have children. But they may as well be flatmates with their partner.

You CANNOT have that soul-connected, heart-connected, intimate relationship when you're staying energetically separate and hiding behind your independence. It's like being in a relationship that has an inbuilt wall of protection around it.
So why do women do this? Basically, it's a coping mechanism that means they don't have to let go. They don't have to be vulnerable

with their whole hearts.

I know many women wear their independence like it's a badge of honor. But to me, it's actually a dark prison cell. And being in a soulmate relationship is the direct opposite of that. Let that sink in for a minute.

Right now, you have an opportunity to give up the word 'independence'. Give up your association with it, and give up its appeal factor. Realize that because of your commitment and loyalty to independence, you've been missing out on your soulmate. And you'll keep on missing out every day that you don't solve this.

YOUR BODYGUARDS ARE SO GOOD THEY NEED ANNUAL LEAVE!

One of the side effects of being 'independent' is that you go out into the world with about 54 bodyguards surrounding you 24/7. They're like your personal suit of armor against love. And they're constantly on the lookout for things to go wrong, so they can keep you safe.

These bodyguards are the best of the best. They're so good at their job that Buckingham palace is trying to recruit them. You employed them and trained them up to keep you independent and ensure that you wouldn't get hurt anymore. Your little girl set them up as protection for her heart, and now they're there, protecting your heart from everything, including love.

Now, let me tell you: your bodyguards are working around the clock for you. And they're insanely loyal, which is wonderful… if you want to stay single.

Think of it this way. Who you truly are is a fucking epic, powerful, majestic Queen. You live in a magnificent palace and those 54 bodyguards surround it. They keep the drawbridge up so no one gets in. Meanwhile, you only live in two of the rooms of that palace. And any man who wants to come and meet you can't get past the bodyguards, let alone walk over the drawbridge.

He just doesn't have a chance.

That palace is your consciousness. You're only using two rooms of it, because those rooms feel safe and they're the known. To step into your true Queen essence, you need to fire your bodyguards, lower the drawbridge and get your staff to open the door when your King comes knocking. You also need to get excited about using the other rooms in your palace. You need to open up to new experiences.

Queens don't hide. They don't play small.
They don't live in fear.

Queens live with their hearts open, ready to receive on every level. They take up all the space and look for the magic and the joy in every moment.

WATCH OUT FOR OVER-TRUSTING THOUGH

I used to think that I was so trusting with my heart. I thought, *"I just don't get it. I trust people 100%. I wear my heart on my sleeve. Isn't that a good thing?"*

But you know what? Actually, it's NOT a good thing. Over-trusting is just as bad as not trusting at all.

I want you to fully take that in.

Over-trusting - just trusting and seeing the good in everyone - has no boundaries. It has no discernment. It also perpetuates your need for bodyguards. How? When you over-trust, you run around seeing the best in people at a surface level. Deep down though, you don't really trust at all. You're just being optimistic and hoping for the best.

Then, sure as shit, something goes wrong and you think, "See I trusted? Love never works out for me! I end up getting hurt!" And your bodyguards' existence is justified. Then the cycle starts all over again.

Just as not trusting keeps you completely guarded and protected with the Great Wall of China around you, trusting too much means you have no clear boundaries. That means people walk all over you, and you put your self-worth in the hands of the people you're dating.

Can you see why over-trusting will never land you your soulmate either?

INTERDEPENDENCE IS THE SECRET INGREDIENT

So your inner control freak is probably wondering how the hell to show up in a relationship now that you know independence is keeping your King out of your life. The answer is that being interdependent within a relationship is the secret ingredient that'll serve you for a lifetime of love. It's the key dynamic in every successful, healthy soulmate relationship.

Don't confuse it with co-dependence, which is an intensely unhealthy relationship pattern. Co-dependence means you and your partner rely excessively on each other. You enable each others' wounds, and depend on each other to fill your own voids.

Interdependence, on the other hand, is a healthy co-existence where you both show up with your hearts and whole selves from a full place. It's a relationship where you both take responsibility for your internal stuff, and you've both already dealt with and removed your own armor.

YOUR SOULMATE RELATIONSHIP
WILL BE PERFECT FOR YOU

Here's the deal: I am a powerful woman. I don't want anyone clipping my wings – no, thank you! I've had plenty of men tell me that I was too much, too intense or too intimidating. They wanted me just to chill the fuck out, and not to take up too much space.

Now obviously, that kind of relationship is like a death sentence to me. So if you're nervous about giving up your bodyguards, I absolutely feel you. I want you to know that I understand exactly how you're feeling. I understand that the idea of interdependence is TERRIFYING, because you're so bloody scared that if you allow a man into your life, he'll just come and strip you of who you are.

But I promise you, divine woman, that when you're truly interdependent, that's not what happens. I can say this with confidence because I'm married to the love of my life, and we're interdependent within our relationship. And you know what? I've been my unapologetic self in this relationship from Day 1.

As you'll know from previous chapters though, I wasn't always like this. I used to leave myself at the door (remember Sonya?) I'd people-please like a big ol' chameleon. And it kept me out of the one thing I wanted more than anything else, which was to be in a heart-connected relationship.

In my relationship now though, I'm in my power more than I've ever been. My amazing soulmate wants me to soar. He wants me to spread my wings. He was attracted to me

> *because I was totally, 100% me, and I shone my light. I'd filled up my own love tank. I knew who I was, and I backed the brilliant woman that is me.*
>
> *And even though I'm interdependent, I STILL fill up my own love tank in our marriage. It's so important to get this relationship dialed in with yourself before you meet your man, because filling up your own tank never stops.*

That's the message that I want you to hear right now, beautiful woman. I'm not asking you to give up who you are. In fact, I'm inviting you to step into who you really are. Because the independent version of yourself is only about one-tenth of who you really are.

"BUT I DON'T WANT TO BE A BURDEN!"

I know so many women who are flat-out terrified of being a burden. When this shows up, it can look like:

- Not taking up space with emotions, needs or energy.
- Staying insular and not putting themselves out there.
- Not wanting to inconvenience anyone or be demanding in any way.

These women would much rather take care of their own needs, because letting someone else do that just feels way too fucking scary and unsafe.

If this is you, divine one, I want you to know that it's super-common to feel like a burden. But doing everything you can to avoid it won't get you any closer to your King.

That's because your King wants you to take up space. He wants you to be all of who you are. He doesn't want you to cry in private. He wants to be there for you, for everything - the good and the bad. He's ALL IN.

So to speed up attracting in that epic man, you need to drop that 'not wanting to be a burden' paradigm. Instead, replace it with a new belief that it's your birthright to be supported. It's your birthright to take up all the space.

*The right man for you will love you
when you show up as you – all of you!*

ATTRACTING A SOULMATE RELATIONSHIP STARTS WITH YOU

To attract in a soulmate relationship with a man, you need first to be in a delicious soulmate relationship with your own majesty. You need to get into a deep, heart-and-soul-connected relationship with yourself. You need to feel your full power. You need to take the time to truly love and honor yourself, and set up healthy boundaries.

Then and ONLY then can you know, in your bones, when the right person is in front of you. Because when you finally learn how to trust and love yourself, the Law of Attraction kicks in. In that moment, you're a vibrational match to let the relationship in fully. You won't worry about whether this person will hurt you, because you've already created the foundation where you know you've got your own back, no matter what.

This means taking the emphasis off the fricking man or relationship completing you, because you're completing yourself first.

You're loving yourself first.

You're honoring yourself first.

You can't do this without setting up a brand-new way of being - a brand-new foundation. You need to set up new boundaries, and a whole new emotional home.

> *Remember: you don't get what*
> *you're worth. You get what you expect.*

You have to admit to yourself that you've been expecting love to fail. You need to be aware that you've been collecting shitty references from failed marriages - perhaps from your own parents' marriage or friends' unhealthy marriages.

And if you've been saying, "I don't want to get married and have children," you need to check in and see whether that's actually your own truth. It *might* be - but it also might just be that your little girl gave up on her dream a long time ago. And if the second one is true? Then, sister, it's time to get that dream back!

But first, you need to thank your bodyguards and release them, one by one, so you can be available, open and ready to receive a relationship right NOW. Not next year. Not next month. NOW.

I'm not going to sugar-coat this. This is not a walk in the park. It's not for the faint-hearted. You're going to need to pull your finger out of your gorgeous ass and commit to what you want like your life depends on it, because it does. Your bodyguards have worked tirelessly for years to keep you and your little girl 'safe'. So shit is about to get real in the best possible way!

You're reading this book because you want love in your life, right? Well, I'm here to tell you that love is your birthright. You can absolutely have it. But you'll need to step up and cut out all the 'I can't's and the excuses and the blaming things outside of you. Remember: your word is your wand.

What you focus on and let into your Vortex is exactly what you'll attract. So get excited: you're about to see how damn powerful you are. When you choose to focus your energy on the things that make you feel good and that you want more of, that's what you'll get.

There are no shortcuts, though. You'll have to be disciplined with yourself. You'll also have to get conscious and present every single moment of every single day, and intentionally focus on what you want instead of focusing on what you don't have. You'll have to choose new, high-vibrational thoughts, beliefs, behaviors and habits to fill your Vortex with - ones that align with a woman who believes in herself and in love.

> *That woman trusts herself, she trusts*
> *love and, of course, she trusts men.*

This is an amazingly expansive consciousness, and it's something that's available to you today if you choose to let it in. It's available if you can flex that new belief muscle every single day like your life depends on it (because, once again, it does).

You need to realize - as I did - that you aren't your past. I had to accept that I wasn't my abandonment. I had to accept that, just because my father died, it didn't mean that all men would leave me. And that acceptance set me free.

Once I'd realized this, I started to put all my thoughts and focus and intention into a few very simple affirmations. I affirmed that:

- "I am soulmate material."
- "Men choose me."
- "Men want to marry me."
- "Men prioritize me because I prioritize me."
- "Men love me because I love me."

Then I started to develop and cultivate this brand-new relationship with myself at the ripe old age of 31. And let me tell you, I haven't looked back. Because of that powerful decision, I knew I could change my life. I wasn't willing to keep feeding my past bullshit, my past story and my past identity.

And because of that, I could create a new one.

So divine woman, I'm giving you a freedom pass right here and now. You know that there's another way to live. You know that there's another identity that will serve you - one that aligns with a woman who does let love in and who is the chosen one.

After all, I know that's why you're reading this book.

THE GOLD NUGGETS

Beautiful woman, we've covered some gold together in the last few pages. Here's a quick recap of the 24-karat nuggets to take away with you and treasure as you head into the next chapter:

- You may wear your independence as a badge of honor, but it's really a prison cell that's keeping you single.

- Your bodyguards are the safeguards that your little girl has put in place to keep anyone from getting too close to you.

- A Queen doesn't need to surround herself with bodyguards or keep the drawbridge to her castle up - she simply needs strong, clear boundaries.

- You'll only attract your soulmate when you fire your bodyguards and cultivate a deep relationship with your own majesty instead.

- You might attract a man without committing to doing this work, but I guarantee that he won't be your soulmate.

GIFT WORK

Over to you, superstar! Go through the exercises that follow to delve into your Queen self: the self who knows she doesn't need any love armor.

Close your eyes and take a moment to drop into the deeper part of yourself. Put your right hand on your heart, and your left hand on your belly. Give yourself this opportunity to connect with that higher self, that Queen who's living inside of you as you read this. That Queen knows that she's perfectly capable of having a beautiful, soul-connected relationship.

- How does that relationship feel?
- By when do you want it?
- Picture your future self in the present, smiling and getting excited, with everyone around you celebrating your flourishing relationship with the love of your life.

Next, allow yourself to download from the Divine. Ask yourself:

- If I allowed myself to actually be truthful and tuned into my heart, and if there were no limits or 'out of bounds' answers, what would I want for myself?
- If I allowed myself to trust with an open heart and truly let love in, how do I want that relationship to feel and be?
- How would the man in this relationship show up for me? How would he make me feel? How does our future feel?
- What does it feel like for me to be the chosen one? The one who's supported, seen, valued, loved and cherished?

(It feels pretty epic, right? Well, sister, you're in luck because this is 100% available to you once you commit to putting yourself first and doing the work to get into alignment!)

Finally, prioritize a small block of time each morning on your schedule to consciously spend in your Vortex. Really feel into your Queen self, and use some or all of the affirmations below to charge your intention of attracting your soulmate relationship. (Or, of course, feel free to create your own affirmations. The only condition is that they MUST inspire you):

- "I am the chosen one."
- "Love is my birthright."
- "Love is safe."
- "I am lovable."
- "I see the real me, men see the real me, and I fucking love me."
- "I am soulmate material."
- "Men choose me."
- "Men want to marry me."
- "Men prioritize me because I prioritize me."
- "Men love me because I love myself fully and accept myself on all levels."

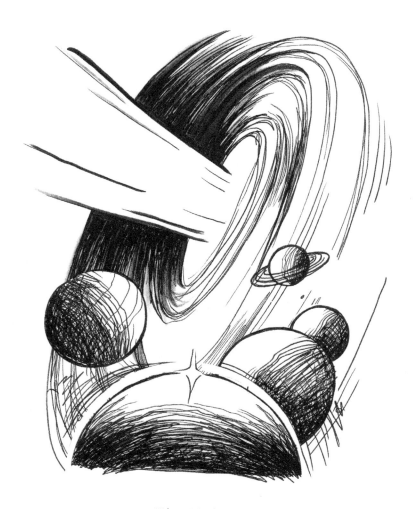

CHAPTER TEN

The Universe

AND HOW

"What we say 'yes' to expands."

Right. You know you need to get the idea of being independent (along with your bodyguards) out of your Vortex. So what's next? Well that, my darling one, all goes back to the stuff we talked about in the first few chapters of the book. Remember: if you focus on how shitty everything is, you'll get more shit. If you focus on the good stuff, you'll get more of that instead.

And THAT's where the Universe comes in. It creates your external world from the way you feel internally - and the way you feel is based on what you choose to believe. So you need to take an active role in managing your beliefs, and commit to doing it in every moment of every day.

Then, after that? Fuck the how - it's none of your business!

LEAVING IT TO THE UNIVERSE IS A BIG OL' TRAP

So many women come to me saying, "Lucy, I'm leaving allll of it to the Universe. I don't want to try too hard. I don't want to push and MAKE things happen. I really just want to leave it all to the Law of Attraction."

Now, there are a couple of giant problems with this, and it's important that we unpack them now. Until you understand them, you won't see what's truly stopping you from attracting your soulmate (even though you feel you're doing everything you possibly can, and then some).

Remember: you might be getting out there and putting on a big smile for the world. But like I said earlier - if deep, deep down, your core belief is that love can't actually happen for you, that's essentially what your Vortex is hardwired to bring you.

You can't fake feelings.

It doesn't matter how many dates you go on, what dress you wear or how vibrant you think you're being. The Universe (AKA the Law of Attraction in action) only ever responds to feelings and your core belief system. We live in a feeling universe. A vibrational universe. And it operates 24/7. That means, no matter how positive or convincing you think you're being, you can't trick the Universe.

I know I've said this before, but that's why, once again, it's not enough to just tick off your 'gratefuls' and affirmations every morning, go to the gym wearing your 'Spiritual Junkie' t-shirt and drink your green juice. That describes SO MANY of the women I talk to.

But when I pull back the curtain, there's no sparkle in their eyes. Their lights have gone out. And it only takes me three minutes to see that they might look stunning on the outside - but they've completely checked out from their hearts and their souls.
They're not feeling much of anything at all.

Back in Chapter 5, we talked about telling yourself that you're 'doing the work' but still not getting the results or outcomes you want in your life. In this case, these women are hiding behind the notion of being spiritual. They're telling themselves that it'll just 'happen when it happens'.

And sister, if you're doing this right now, it's costing you everything. You're sacrificing your future to the notion that the Universe will just bring everything to you.

It won't. The Universe doesn't operate like that. I wish it did.
OK, time for another truthbomb: you need to be clear on what you want. You need to actively participate in co-creating it by getting into alignment with it. And most of all, you need to pay attention to what

you use your Vortex to create. If you don't do all those things? Then beauty, you have zero chance of attracting in the love of your life.

Again, it just doesn't work like that.

YOU'RE HIDING FROM YOURSELF BY LEAVING IT TO THE UNIVERSE

Once again, I get it. I used to say, "I'm doing all the work. I'm a super-spiritual person. I just KNOW that next year will be the year my dreams come true."

But then 'next year' kept rolling into the year after that, and the year after that. Finally, I woke up at 36, after doing ten years of solid work on myself, and it was a seriously rude awakening. I thought, *"I want a family. I want to have babies. I refuse to give up on my dream of being in a soulmate relationship. But whatever I'm doing at the moment is clearly not working. It's obviously not enough for me to just keep saying, 'It's going to happen. I'm really close now.'"*

And, as I've told you, despite all that work, my heart was still closed. Because back then, I still - in my deepest self, my core - didn't believe I was worthy of a soulmate relationship.
That's why it's important to figure out where you're hiding from yourself, and kick that shit to the curb. That's the only way you can get on with expanding into the fullest, most glorious version of your Queen self.

The three main ways I see women hiding from themselves and 'leaving it to the Universe' are by:

- Being 'busy' all the time.
- Being willing to give up.
- Being angry at the Universe for not bringing them what they want.

Let's go deeper into each of these, so you can see where you're hiding and robbing yourself of your epic dream.

HIDING BEHIND BEING 'BUSY'

So many women hide behind being too busy. They say, "I'm leaving it to the Universe, but right now, I've got too much on. Now's just not a good time." Maybe they have to work, or they have a holiday - there's always something.

But here's the thing, divine woman.

You can't AFFORD to be too busy for love.

If you are, you'll never attract your soulmate!

I believe love is the highest currency that we have on this planet. And when you fully let that idea in, it makes sense that love will only make every area of your life ten times better. You'll be able to receive more when you're living in harmony with your true self and in the vibration of love. Period.

(Plus orgasms on tap with someone you're in love with will put you into your highest alignment and frequency. They make you incredibly receptive on all levels. Trust me on this!)

HIDING BEHIND GIVING UP

Other women just give up. They say something like, "Well, I *wanted* children, but I left it to the Universe and it's too late now," or, "Lucy, this just doesn't seem like it'll ever happen!"
If this is you, then I'm here to say, "Don't quit on your dream, but don't just sit there waiting for it to fall into your lap either!" Get conscious. Wake up! Start declaring exactly what it is that you want. Focus your energy on that. Then do the work to believe with every fiber of your being that you already have it.

That's how you change your life, not by passively leaving it to the Universe, then giving up and settling. Settling means you're marinating in spoiled brat, hopeless energy. It's certainly not who you are - it's not you in your Queen energy with your crown on.

HIDING BEHIND BEING PISSED OFF AT THE UNIVERSE

Finally, other women get downright pissed off with the Universe. They say, "I'm pissed off that the Universe is taking so long," or "I'm pissed off with God for not letting me have this relationship!"

If this is you, you feel like you've been 'doing the work' for so long that God or the Universe 'owes' you the results. And you can't understand why you aren't getting them. You're completely perplexed.

Well, epic woman, you're not getting those results because you're not being intentional. You're not doing your part by taking the actions you need to take to actually get your heart open.
Like your sisters above, you're being lazy and passive. And that needs to change ASAP.

YOU NEED TO OWN YOUR POWER

I know. I get it. You haven't got what you wanted yet, so now you're annoyed and looking for something or someone to blame.

But beauty, that is NOT powerful. 'Leaving your future to the Universe' is essentially bailing on yourself. Remember: the Universe only ever responds to what you truly believe. That means it can't give you anything if you believe it's given up on you or forgotten about you. If you feel that, my darling, it's because you've given up on you.

I was pretty devastated when I finally got that. Well, it was devastating... but it was also super-illuminating. I thought, *"OK, this is the missing puzzle piece, and I NEED to prioritize myself and my dream right now."* That was the key to getting into alignment with my power. I had to make it my priority - not something I half-asked for and dabbled with.

I couldn't put all my attention and focus into things that were meaningless to me and then just say, "Oh, I'm leaving the stuff that means the most to me to the Universe."

That's flippant.

It's not powerful at all.

And, as I said, it's a hiding place. You do it because you're still numb. You're in denial. Hiding means you can just keep putting your dreams outside of yourself as something you'll have 'one day when'. It means you don't have to risk anything in the now.
Love is about taking a risk, getting out of your comfort zone and leading with an open heart.

BUT IF I'M NOT LEAVING IT TO THE UNIVERSE... WHAT DO I DO?

If you want to live a lit-up life and thrive, instead of living in this survival paradigm, you'll need to start getting good at taking risks.

You'll also have to start getting good at living on the edge of your heart.

And you'll have to start getting good at being bold.
Because here's the thing. I'm not in a relationship with the love of my life because it just one day, out of the blue, happened to me. It's also not because I'm lucky. Nor is it because I'm pretty. So let's just clear this up:

The Universe responds to clarity.

The Universe also responds to certainty, conviction and belief that you can have whatever you desire. This works across every spectrum, no matter what you're attracting. You can use this principle to attract and manifest a cup of coffee just as easily as you can with attracting in the love of your life.

Either way, you just have to be a vibrational match. You've got to align with being someone who believes that she can absolutely attract love (or a cup of coffee) - and better yet, keep it. Because the Universe responds to your vibration in every single moment, and you have to believe with every fiber of your being that what you want is your birthright.

My dreams only came true because I wasn't willing to tolerate not having them. I wasn't willing to tolerate being passive for one more day and not seeing them become reality. They came true because I recognized that living in hope and wishing for the best is not a strategy.

Hope is NOT a strategy.

(And while we're at it, getting advice from family and friends is not a strategy either.)

Hope might be a gateway to walk through so you can start getting into alignment, but no amount of hoping will ever actually change anything. It's just not going to get you there. And simply sitting and hoping is costing you your health. It's costing you your mental wellbeing. It's costing you your happiness. It may even be costing you the baby you once dreamed of.

At the end of the day, you either fuel your dream with fear, victimhood and hope, or you fuel it with belief and certainty. The choice is yours, and I bet you can guess which option will get you your desired outcome.

IT'S ABOUT PRIORITIZING AND COMMITMENT

On the other side of that 'hope' gateway, you need to be willing to commit to your dreams. You need to prioritize them today as the most important thing in your life.

Now, this isn't about obsessing over your dream to MAKE it happen. I'm not saying that at all. You need to commit to the outcome without getting attached to the 'how'. That's the only way to harness the Law of Attraction. Because when you put your attention and focus into whatever you're out to create? And when you then spend time in your Vortex, genuinely feeling what it's like to have that thing already in your life? THAT, darling one, is when you'll start to see it showing up in your external reality.

To turn your dreams into that reality though, you've got to build belief systems that support your vision. You've got to build a new identity and a whole new foundation that supports it.

In some ways, it's a lot like building a brand-new muscle from scratch. You don't just go to the gym for a single day and expect to get a six-pack, right? It doesn't work like that. You know you need to commit to training consistently, and then you start to see the results.

Well, it's exactly the same with your dreams. You need to step up and play full-out with 100% commitment. And you need to stop tolerating your own excuses.

At the end of this chapter, I've created an exercise for you that I know will push you out of your comfort zone. In it, I ask you to set a date for when you'd love your soulmate relationship to show up in your life.

This might feel a little bit scary, but I want you to put a date on it because that will force you to get into action. It'll force you to start being the woman you need to be. That version of you already knows how to have a soulmate relationship. She's already sitting in her feminine power and her glorious self-worth.
You'll need to step into how that version of you shows up each day, knowing that she can have whatever she desires. Then you'll need to become her right now and get excited about it - because suddenly, when you do, you'll start seeing what you want manifesting.

This is about the long game. It's about having a very clear, very tangible goal of what you want when it comes to love, and then letting yourself feel that way right now. Let yourself feel the joy, the happiness, the love, the support and the connection. Let yourself really feel that someone's got your back.

It's about taking time every day to consciously sit in your Vortex, soaking in those feelings. This might bring you to tears. If so, that's beautiful. As I said in Chapter 5, most of us just don't allow ourselves to feel. We're so busy protecting ourselves and keeping our dream at arm's length that we numb ourselves out as a coping mechanism.

So allow yourself to feel whatever comes up when you visualize having your dream come true. Regularly, consistently sit there in your Vortex, feeling that future you long for here, now, in the present. Be grateful for it right now - and do it as often as possible.

You wouldn't set off to climb Everest without training, would you? Hell no! You'd prepare for it. You'd get your body used to the altitude. You'd get your fitness in good enough condition to handle the steep terrain. You'd get support and learn exactly what the route up the mountain would look like. You'd develop a process so that you knew how to show up as someone who could make it to the top.

And that's exactly what we're talking about here, beauty. You need to get just as serious about what it'll take to shift decades of conditioning so you can create your dream life.

ONCE YOU FEEL IT, YOU'VE GOT TO BELIEVE IN IT

Before I attracted in my beautiful husband, I was doing more than waking up feeling grateful in advance for what I wanted. I was also making sure I believed in the reality that he was already in my life. I could feel him. I was crystal clear on the energy of our relationship. And honestly, I walked around in a dual reality where I didn't feel single anymore. I actually felt his presence.

And let me tell you, when he did show up, it was fast. I set a deadline of three months, and he showed up within two. That's literally how quickly things can change if you refuse to hand your dream over or outsource it to the Universe.

So yes. I mean it when I say that the Universe will meet you when you choose to step up and start to build your conviction and your certainty. It will begin to orchestrate situations for you that you could never have managed singlehandedly. Look: the Universe has created galaxies, mountains and planets. Don't underestimate its power!

When you do your bit and prioritize your dream, you can totally have it. And if you keep going until you're laser-clear and vibrating with its energy, that's when everything shows up. You need to energetically create the space for your dream to come into your life.

It doesn't matter if you have a lot of plates in the air. What matters is that you energetically prioritize this dream and prioritize the FEELING and believing time as part of your everyday ritual.

FUCK THE 'HOW' – THAT'S NONE OF YOUR BUSINESS

I know I've said that you have to be prepared to commit to your dreams. You have to be prepared to prioritize them.
But it's tempting to think that means focusing on 'the how'. That's natural. As humans, once we have a destination, we want to know how we'll get there. And while that works in business if you're in the corporate world or you're an entrepreneur - it does NOT work when it comes to your dreams.

Yes, sure we need our masculine: the do, do, do part of ourselves that I've talked about in earlier chapters. We need to get into that action mode and get proactive. But when it comes to love - or any other outcome you dream of - you cannot possibly insist on knowing how to get to the outcome you want in advance.
Your dreams are about doing the deep inner work to connect with what it is that you want and how that makes you feel - all the things we've talked about in this chapter. After that, you've got to invite in surrender. And this, divine woman...

This is where you bring the Universe in.

You 'hand your dreams over to the Universe' AFTER you've done your work. And your work - remember - is to open your heart, deeply heal that inner little girl and dissolve her abandonment issues and not-enough-ness. It's to create a brand-new mindset, a brand-new belief system, brand-new behaviors and brand-new boundaries that will serve you.

Only once you've done all that can you step into alignment with being a woman who will absolutely have a soulmate relationship (or whatever else you're dreaming of). Only then can you keep that relationship from a place of ease and flow, versus trying to hold on to it.

This is being intentional with 'leaving it to the Universe'. It's using the Law of Attraction the way it was designed: getting very clear on your desire and expecting to receive it.

After that, it's about getting out of the way without asking how it's going to happen. Here's an example of a time I did exactly that...

I LET THE UNIVERSE TAKE
CARE OF THE 'HOW'...

When I got really, really clear that I still hadn't opened my heart, I knew I needed to get the right support. I made it my absolute mission, even though I was flat-out with my one-woman, off-Broadway show.

Although I was extremely busy and barely had any time in my schedule, I made room in my consciousness for my soulmate to come in. I was 36 and I wanted a family. So I made doing the work a non-negotiable for me and told myself, "Lucy, if you don't make this your top priority this instant, it's never going to happen."

I knew there would never be a 'right time' unless I made it the right time.

So I just did my bit with deeply loving myself each day. I looked into the mirror every single morning, and spent time being with myself and loving myself on every level. I smiled at my reflection and said, "Hello, beautiful woman. I love you. I see you. I'm so proud of you. And I'm so excited that you are with the love of your life."

I want to be clear that I wasn't just looking at myself. I was truly being with myself and seeing myself fully. It made me emotional when I first started to do this because I realized how disconnected I'd been from myself for way too long.

This helped to re-educate my cells that I deserved love and was an expert at receiving it. I committed to consistently doing this with a kind of light-hearted energy – and I had a ball doing it.

I made it an absolute reality that love was coming into my life. I shared it with my friends (some of whom, as I've said before, thought I was batshit crazy). They said, "But Lucy, you're not even online at the moment. How on earth do you expect to attract love in?"

I replied, "That's exactly right. It's coming BECAUSE I'm expecting it."

That stopped them in their tracks. A couple of people gave me those 'watch this space' looks. Others actually said, "Well, this'll be interesting!"

I just told them, "Keep watching. You'll see."

In addition to that, I've already mentioned in previous chapters how discerning I became about who I surrounded myself with. I've told you about no longer going on brunch dates with girlfriends who kept talking about how hopeless and hard love is. And I've also told you how I literally removed myself from any conversations that didn't align with what I was out to create.

But I also made sure I allowed in references and stories of things that were in alignment. I kept looking at the sort of relationships that I wanted, and surrounding myself with friends who were in those kinds of healthy relationships. To be honest, it was far more fun to hang out with them than to be in that negative energy anyway. But I treated the mindset work like it was life or death.

And that got me into alignment fast.

> *Once I'd done all that work, I left EVERYTHING else up to the Universe. I didn't know how my soulmate would show up, and I didn't need to. I didn't worry about it. I wasn't online trying to make him show up – in fact, I was putting all my energy and passion into my show.*
>
> *Because you know the result: two months later, right before my show started, I met that soulmate. He held a huge space for me during the show, and I don't know how I'd have gotten through it without him.*

The point of my story is that I didn't have to do anything. I had conversations with the Universe every day, where I said, "You're going to bring me my man, and the right circumstance to meet him in." I got very clear on how I wanted to feel in our relationship.

And then I really felt his energy and my gratitude for it as I thanked the Universe every day for bringing me that divine man.

So even though I was insanely busy, I prioritized letting love in, which means I accepted any invitations that came my way. I knew I had to meet the Universe halfway, even if I was exhausted. My dream man wouldn't just show up at my house, especially during the busiest time of my life.

You've already read the story of how I met him - the party that I didn't feel like going to, and schlepping all the way uptown in the middle of winter. But I went, because connecting with my soulmate was my priority.

And that was the only reason I could end up meeting him.

CONTROL FREAK ENERGY SHOWS THAT
YOU DON'T TRUST THE UNIVERSE

When Tully first came to work with me, she was totally in her masculine, independent identity. She was a control freak who didn't trust love, men or relationships, because deep inside, she didn't trust herself to hold down a relationship. She didn't think she was worthy of that kind of love, and she was riddled with self- doubt. She just didn't believe that she could have it.

Tully felt lost. Underneath her massive public persona and the smile she showed to the world, she constantly worried that there must be something wrong with her. She was ashamed and felt like a failure. She spent most days overwhelmed, with a sinking feeling in the pit of her stomach.

And she felt like, no matter how much she wanted this amazing relationship, it was slipping further and further away from her. Every day that she spent single felt meaningless, and the idea of ending up alone was like a death sentence.

In fact, she already felt dead inside.

When we started working together, I told her she needed to get connected back into her heart. She had to consciously spend time in her Vortex feeling what she wanted to create in her life instead of recycling the status quo.

That was challenging for Tully, and she resisted giving up control of the HOW. But she overcame her resistance, hunkered down and committed to the work. She managed to connect with the deepest part of herself – her feminine power and her vulnerability – and she fucking loved it.

For the first time in her life, she focused fully on attracting in what she wanted and left the how up to the Universe. She'd done a shitload of self-development before working with me, but she'd never been able to connect with her heart at this level. And – like so many of my other clients – she was also blown away by her own power.

Fast forward to now, and Tully's with the love of her life. He adores her, and she can't believe that she'd completely given up on love just six months ago.

She emailed me recently to tell me how grateful she is to have done this work and how proud of herself she is. In her email, she said that her whole soul feels revitalized. She feels like a completely different person now – as though she's finally being the woman she was born to be. She's talking about kids with her man, and has just moved in with him. Not only that, but her big dreams of winning an Oscar for directing feel closer than ever, and she feels like a brand-new woman.

These two stories clearly demonstrate the importance of giving up trying to figure out the 'how'. When I was calling in my soulmate, I had to give up trying to *make* it happen.
Just like Tully, I had to give up control.

And when I truly got that and saw the rapid results in my love life, I knew for sure that the Universe is far more capable of bringing me my desires than I am. So I started using the same process with everything I dreamed of, which is now my soulmate formula.
Again, what I want you to hear right now is that YOUR job is to take care of your vibration and do the inner work. The Universe *wants*

you to experience deep, soul-connected love (and anything else you dream of). But you've got to take ownership. You've got to realize how powerful you are. You've got to realize that you co-create together with the Universe.

When you do this, life starts to get amazing and expansive. You start to realize how 'not alone' you are. You realize you're being guided and supported in every single moment. You discover that you know exactly what (if anything) you have to do - and then all that's left is to do it, get out of the way, hand your dream over and get ready to receive.

Right now, you're the only one who's cutting yourself off from constant abundance. You're the only one stopping yourself because you've been committed to living out of a fear paradigm and feeling unworthy and undeserving. You've put all your attention onto those things instead of recognizing yourself as the powerful creator that you are. You've talked yourself out of love instead of talking yourself into it.

'How' your dreams will manifest is simply none of your business. It never has been and it never will be. But what is your business and your responsibility is falling madly, deeply, head-over-heels in love with yourself. It's refusing to allow anyone to shit in your Vortex. And it's choosing now as the right time for you to let love in.

Because why the fuck not you? Get honest with yourself. If not now, then when WILL be the right time?

Fortune favors the bold

And sister, if all of this makes you scared as hell, I've got you. Next, we'll talk about the v-word, vulnerability. And you'll learn how being vulnerable is your superpower.

THE GOLD NUGGETS

Beautiful woman, we've covered some gold together in the last few pages. Here's a quick recap of the 24-karat nuggets to take away with you and treasure as you head into the next chapter:

- It's tempting to just 'leave everything up to the Universe', but that's a trap.

- It's a way of hiding from yourself that leads to giving up on your dreams and leaves you pissed off at the Universe when it doesn't deliver.

- The Universe responds to clarity and feelings, which are based in your beliefs.

- Once you're committed to doing the work to create beliefs that empower you, you need to give up the 'how', hand it over and build your faith muscle.

GIFT WORK

Over to you, superstar! Go through the exercise below to let go of the 'how' so that you can attract your soulmate.

Close your eyes and imagine you have a fairy godmother who's standing right in front of you. She's here to grant you a wish. When she asks you what it is, let your highest self - that inner Queen who knows a soulmate relationship is her birthright - answer.

Now I want you to write down a date. When would you love to have this soulmate relationship in your life? Don't worry about the how. That's none of your business. When would you love to have it?

When would feel really juicy and exciting for you?

Finally, ditch the checklist, gorgeous! Your checklist is keeping you in your head. Instead, use the power of your limitless imagination and belief to bring in everything you desire. Take your journal, write out your answers to the prompts below and let yourself FEEL all of it. It's time to receive!

- Describe the energy of the man you want to magnetize. What are his qualities? Take a moment to feel into this. How does he make you feel?
- What do you do together? How does it feel having this man in your life?
- What life are you creating together? How does that make you feel?

Remember, it's all about how this makes you feel, so write from your heart, not your head.

You've got this, darling woman!

CHAPTER ELEVEN

VULNERABILITY

"It's time to get real with yourself and the world."

You're doing the work in your Vortex, and you've given over 'the how' to the Universe. Fantastic! But if you're not in a soulmate relationship, there's something more going on.

For many of the women I work with, that 'something' is vulnerability – because unless you can be vulnerable, you'll sabotage all your efforts. The problem is that most people think they're being vulnerable when they're actually being needy AF. And divine woman, being needy and being vulnerable are in completely different universes from each other.

So in this chapter, we'll talk about how opening your heart is an inside job. We'll look at what being vulnerable looks like in real time, and why you set yourself up to fail if you're not willing to plug into your stunning vulnerability.

VULNERABILITY VS. NEEDINESS

The good news is that vulnerability isn't what you think it is.
So many divine women who come to me complain, "Lucy, I just don't get it. I'm vulnerable, I'm bringing myself into these relationships. Yet the men I like don't hang around. They start off super-interested, but then they go cold. They don't choose me. They don't commit to me."

Here's the bottom line: vulnerability so often gets misinterpreted for its poor cousin, neediness. Women think they're being vulnerable by simply saying what they want in a relationship. But in reality, doing that can be very needy. It can come from an insecure place where what you truly want is to know whether the guy likes you. You're desperate to know whether he wants to move things to the next level.

When you do this, it comes from lack and fear, and it's palpable. Men can smell your neediness, just as much as you can smell when a man is being needy with you. And it's a complete turnoff for them. It's like a repellent. It's like you're walking around with this fragrance that's pushing away the guy, because you're not expressing your uninhibited truth. You're putting far too much energy into caring what he thinks of you instead of feeling into what you think of you.

Let's look at the difference in detail.

- **Neediness** is you projecting all your fear, panic and doubt about what could go wrong in the relationship. You're so scared that what you're really asking him is, "Hey, are you serious about me? When are we going to get married? Do you want to have children?"

That's a mechanical approach to the relationship. It's completely masculine and cerebral. It's from that part of you that just wants instant answers and outcomes, so it means you come from fear and zero trust in the relationship unfolding organically.

- **Vulnerability**, on the other hand, is you connecting with that powerful feminine intuition - that deep knowing in your heart space - and then expressing it. You don't need to ask someone whether they're into you or where the relationship is going. Instead, you trust yourself and tune in to your own heart. You ask yourself, "Hey, does this feel good for me?" and wait for your heart to respond. Then you act from that place of inner knowing.

This then means you can sit in your feminine power and tell the guy, "Hey, this is where I see us now, and I want to go to the next level. Is that what you want too?" If he replies, "No", you can thank him for being honest and move on. You can bless and release that relationship to make room for the King who's waiting for you. Because beautiful woman, **your inner Queen self knows that there's an abundance of Kings, and she doesn't need to try to make something work.**

I used to think that I was being vulnerable. I used to think I was self-expressed. I used to think I was so authentic. And it used to utterly confuse the crap out of me, because I still wasn't getting what I wanted out of my relationships.

I had enough people telling me, "Hey Lucy, you're a great catch!" I knew I didn't have a face like a smashed crab or the back of a sandshoe. And yet still, my dates just evaporated. I remember thinking, "*I don't understand it. Maybe I'm just not good at love.*" I'm sure you've had those thoughts yourself. Or perhaps you've thought:

- "*Maybe I'm not meant to be in a relationship. I'm just not good at it.*"
- "*I'm a free spirit.*" (You might recognize this as another one of mine!)
- "*Whenever I'm vulnerable, it never gets received the right way.*"
- "*Men just don't get me - they can't handle me.*"

We all have moments in a relationship where it starts to cross the border from getting to know each other into, "*Holy shit, I like this person and now I have no idea who to be.*" Maybe for you, that's on Date 5, or at Month 3. Either way, sound familiar?

That was what used to happen to me. I'd be cool on the first and second date. But then the third date started to get a bit wobbly. By the fourth date, I was starting to panic. And by Date 5, Lucy was nowhere to be seen. She'd run off to Alaska, and Sonya (remember her from Chapter 7?) had suddenly shown up to take her place. Meanwhile, the guy I was going out with was like, "Hang on a minute, I thought I had a date with Lucy. Who the hell is this woman?"

Can you see yourself in this story? It's pretty funny, but this is what so many women do, and then they get perplexed about why love just doesn't work. If you're like them, you need a new story: that love does work for you. But to have love work for you, you've got to do whatever it takes to make being vulnerable your absolute priority.

You have to lead with your stunning vulnerability and be proud of it, instead of very occasionally bringing it out from a place of shame and insecurity.

I went through life for 30 years hiding my vulnerability. I clung to being strong and independent (see Chapter 9 for more on that). I clung to having everything together, not dropping the ball and DEFINITELY not burdening anyone with my emotions and feelings.

Then, on about the third date in any relationship, I'd just hand over my power. I'd start to sink into this horrible feeling of not knowing where I stood. That's when my insecurity would kick into high gear. I'd feel sick in the pit of my stomach. I'd let the guy call the shots, and I wouldn't dare to ask for what I wanted.

For example, I'd never instigate texts. I'd just respond when he messaged, and then overanalyze each text like a crazy person. I'd feel like I had to ask those questions I didn't want to ask about where the relationship was going and whether he was serious.

If you've been there, you know it feels like absolute crap, right? Because it comes from such an insecure place.

I want you to let this land deep. Without true vulnerability, you cannot have a high-vibrational soulmate relationship. And I hear you asking, "Okay, Lucy, that sounds great. But how do I actually do that in a relationship when I thought I was being vulnerable?"

So let's crack the lid wide open on what that kind of true vulnerability looks like, and how it's different from neediness.

Real vulnerability is speaking from your heart, in the strength and self-assurance of your Queen self's power. Neediness is telling your man what you want from that super-masculine ultimatum place because you need to control what's happening. It's operating from that horrible, insecure place of overcompensation, trying too hard and betraying your own boundaries. You do it because, deep down, you're terrified the relationship is going to end, so that's your focus.

This leaves the guy holding all the cards, and leaves you feeling even more worthless. And then, yep, he starts to pull away like clockwork, and it ends shortly afterward 'like it always does' because that's what you're wired to expect.

That kind of 'vulnerability' doesn't feel good, because it's not true vulnerability. It's just scarcity and neediness and your scared inner little girl running the show. It's leaving yourself at the door and sabotaging your relationships one after the other. It's hiding behind masks and protection and game-playing, which never ends well. It's not even in the same stratosphere as true vulnerability.

And beauty? That definition of vulnerability SUCKS balls!

BRENÉ BROWN WAS RIGHT

My revelation about vulnerability came when I followed my heart all the way to New York to act. It was 2011, and Brene Brown's TED talk about vulnerability was going viral.

When I watched her video, my eyes were on stalks! I'd never heard anything like it. Her words had me buzzing for days, because I felt the truth of what vulnerability was for the first time in my life. I still had to integrate it, but I got the taste and I wanted more.

Then, during the same time period, I went to audition at a top acting studio in New York City with Susan Batson, who coaches Nicole Kidman and many other big stars. Susan saw my audition and said, "You're technically very good, Lucy."

I asked, "What do you mean, technically?"

She replied, "You've clearly got the gift, but there's absolutely no vulnerability coming from you. When you tap into your vulnerability though, look out, Cate Blanchett!"

That got me pumped to explore my vulnerability, but I felt like she could have been speaking Egyptian. So I asked her how I could access this vulnerability, and she told me, "You don't connect with your heart when you act. You don't share the depth of who you are or connect to what you're saying at any kind of deep level. When you find a way to connect, it's going to be a game-changer, but you're going to have to let us see and feel you, Lucy."

I decided right then that I'd figure out how to connect with my heart as I acted no matter what... But then I looked around my life and started to join the dots. I realized that my lack of vulnerability was ALSO showing up in all the relationships I had with men. It was such an AHA moment, and I'll always remember it as a turning point for me.

Susan's words truly were the biggest gift. I started to get excited about what vulnerability meant, and about who I could be in the world if I was willing to commit to it.

I knew I needed to be willing to expose my heart and to bring the real, uninhibited Lucy into this life. I needed to stop fearing rejection and worrying about how I'd be received or judged. Instead, I just needed to stay true to that full divine self-expression that lived inside of me. I'd been keeping it in a cage, and I needed to set it free.

VULNERABILITY IS YOUR SUPERPOWER

I want to give you a whole new context around vulnerability, and I want you to let that context seriously excite you. I want you to see being vulnerable as a superpower, and know that you can't do love without it.

Being vulnerable takes courage and full faith in yourself. It takes standing in and completely owning your glorious feminine power - ALL of it. But in order to do this, you need to know yourself fully. You need to know what you like and what you don't like. You need to know your non-negotiables, and not be afraid to share your heart, your soul and your dreams with that special person.
It requires not holding back your self-expression and unapologetically giving yourself permission to be ALL of who you are. It requires plugging into your deserve-ability and your power. And sister, walking around in that kind of vulnerability is like wearing a fragrance called 'Magnetism' with a capital 'M' that's stronger and more potent than any Chanel perfume. Trust me: you don't need perfume when you're plugged into your vulnerability.

Unfortunately, in our society, we're not taught to express ourselves unapologetically.

We're not taught to take up space.

If anything, we're told, "Keep a lid on it. Don't be too much. Don't say too much."

Before I connected the dots, I'd dimmed my light for so damn long that I didn't know how to be me. Then, suddenly, I was hearing the exact opposite from everywhere: "You've got to be who you really are. You've got to bring who you really are into this world if you want to live on purpose, connect with your gifts and truly experience love."

That sounded terrifying, but it also sounded exhilarating because I knew that it was within reach.

And I want you to get right now that you can activate your vulnerability just by choosing to. You can decide as a new non-negotiable that you'll never again attempt love without your vulnerability. And you can make a sacred vow to yourself that you'll commit to doing whatever it takes to open your heart and keep it open, no matter what.

And yes, divine one, 'keeping your heart open' is a key part of the process. I see so many women open their hearts, but then, when they get rejected, BOOM... they close down again for good. They aren't brave enough to keep their hearts open after rejection, and that needs to change if they want a soulmate relationship.

BRAVADO ISN'T VULNERABILITY

When Trish started working with me, she was stuck in an infatuation cycle where she put men up on pedestals. She was also living from her masculine with a kickass career and a shitload of love armor, and even the mention of 'the v-word' scared the crap out of her.

She thought she was being responsible and doing her due diligence when she asked men about their intentions and stated her needs upfront. But it was all completely transactional. She led with that energy of bravado and 'I've got this' that we talked about back in Chapter 9.

Trish's MO was that she didn't need a man because she was strong and independent. She'd tell her girlfriends (and convince herself) that men just couldn't handle her. Quietly though, she started to question whether or not she was even meant to have the relationship of her dreams.

In fact, by the time Trish came to me, she'd already given up on having a soulmate relationship. But when she did my Soul to Soul program, she dug way down deep into her soul and activated her divine feminine and her heart.

That looked incredible on her. It softened her masculine front, and she started to bloom like the most gorgeous rose you've ever seen. The other women in the program with her cheered her on as she had her massive AHA moment. She realized that she'd never given herself permission to be her true self, and that it all stemmed back to never feeling seen by her mother.

> *Once she finally healed this wound, she started connecting to the deepest part of her soul, and she slowly came home to her truest essence. It was amazing to witness her getting lit up by her own light.*
>
> *And now, today, she's with her soulmate, who she met online during the coronavirus pandemic. She's so proud of the woman she's become: a Queen who trusts herself in love and lets people see who she truly is without putting on her false confidence and bravado front.*
>
> *And yes, she loves being vulnerable now.*

CLOSING YOUR HEART STIFLES YOUR POWER

Woman to woman, I'm here to tell you that we can't afford to give our power away by closing our hearts. And we don't have to.
I wish someone had told me this way back when. I spent many years keeping my heart closed because of my inbuilt belief that, *"I'm too sensitive, and vulnerability's scary."* But of course, I wasn't being vulnerable from a place of power.

What I thought was vulnerability was just my inner little girl expressing herself from her dense, limited, undeserving place. Deep down, she didn't expect love to work out. She expected to be left and abandoned (just like with my dad). So I subconsciously attracted men who weren't ready, and who didn't choose me, because that's what I expected and what felt safe.

And so that was my whole worldview. That was what I plugged into. It was what I brought into my Vortex. As a result, my subconscious expectations kept me single and stuck in Groundhog Day.

If the same thing is true for you, sister, then I want you to drop the story that you're damaged goods because of what has happened to you. Like we've talked about before: your mindset and conditioning are the issue. Not you!

VULNERABILITY IN REAL TIME

Have you ever been in that space where you asked the man, "Hey, where's this relationship going?" As we've talked about earlier in the chapter, that's usually neediness. It's not you being in your feminine. Instead, it's your little girl coming from fear, lack and unworthiness.

True vulnerability is about trusting that the timing's right when you start to have all the feelings. You might notice that sabotage is knocking on your door - that you're seriously into this person, but you're not sure where you stand.

When that instinct comes up, it's vital to remind yourself that you're in this relationship on your terms, not someone else's. It's up to YOU whether you choose to move forward with this relationship or not - got that?

You need to know that YOU hold all the cards.

Really take a moment to let that truth in. You're not waiting to find out whether the guy is ready for you. Instead, you're checking in to ask yourself, "Is this relationship aligned with where I'm going?" and *"Does it feel good for me to be around this person?"*

That's a very, very different energy and focus compared to, *"Is this relationship OK with him? Is it what he wants?"*

This is about you being crystal clear on what you want. Then it's about having the courage to check in with him to see whether his response is a, "Yes, let's explore it," or a, "No thanks, I'm out." In a conversation, that check-in might look something like, "Hey Matt, I have to be honest. I'm loving hanging out with you and I'm starting to develop some pretty awesome feelings. I want to check in and see if we're on the same page. How do you feel?"

Now, here's where the true vulnerability comes in: you have to open your heart enough to receive his answer, whatever it might be.

Matt might say, "Yes, I'm so with you. I was actually having the exact same feelings! I was even thinking about us moving in together." If so, then BOOM, you're on track.

But what if he turns around and says, "Oh, I really like you, but I'll be honest, I don't want anything serious."? In that case, you, my darling, have a choice to make. You need to ask yourself, *"Does this suit me? Is this OK with me? Am I OK to wait for Matt to catch up?"*

If you're genuinely, deep-down-on-a-soul-level fine with it, you can say so. Or, if time is of the essence, you can thank Matt for his truth by saying something like, "You know what, Matt? Thank you so much for being honest. I totally dig that. But I'll be honest with you in return that I know what I want. Like I said, I like you. And if you're just not where I am, that's totally cool. Let's respect each other's time though and wrap this thing up: I'm ready now and I'm not willing to wait for you, because I know you might never be ready."

What makes this light-years apart from neediness is that you're standing in your feminine power and worthiness. So if he says, "Umm, no, I'm not on the same page," you don't let your entire world crumble. Sure, you might be disappointed and sad for a while, but you're not there trying to make your relationship with him 'THE' relationship. You're not trying to make Matt into 'The One'.

Instead, you're being a true Queen who has an abundance mindset, and who just says, "Next!" You're not pinning all your sense of worth or deserve-ability (or your future and dreams) on this one freaking person's schedule.

And THAT, divine woman, is vulnerability from a place of power. It takes real courage to listen to and accept someone else's truth. It takes courage not to fall into a heap, crying, "How could you spend all this time with me, and talk about all these amazing things with no intention of committing to me?"

But when you respond like that, you're playing the victim. You're being your little girl. When you come from that place, what's actually running the show is all your abandonment and wounding. And remember: you can't have a soulmate relationship with your little girl running the show.

This is often why men ghost. It's not because they're all assholes. Yes, being ghosted doesn't feel great, but you can make it into a good thing. You can use it to take responsibility and look at yourself, instead of shelving the blame outside of yourself. Blaming men is no different from blaming your age, the city you live in, your childhood, your parents, the government or your weight.

And when you stop blaming and own your circumstances, you can change them. You can start getting what you do want instead of complaining about getting what you don't.

So rather than sitting there in that relationship you're not happy with, waiting like a puppy for him to be ready, you can take responsibility. You can leave that relationship, and then get back to your big, juicy dream, knowing deep in your heart that your King is on his way.

This is an abundance mindset. It takes courage to listen to and be with the truth that a relationship isn't working. But when you love and value yourself, you aren't scared of it. You know how to move through it with grace, respect and reverence - both for yourself and for the other person. Bless and release that guy, then get your butt out of that relationship already, because your King awaits!

I want you to see how empowered you are when you love yourself enough to instigate this conversation without depending on a particular outcome. If it's not what you were hoping for, you can just say, "Thank you, next!" and know that the Universe is redirecting you. You know you're now available for a man who IS aligned and ready to rock! And you know you're creating a new foundation that's built on solid faith, belief and a deep knowing that love does work out for you.

This allows you to get back onto your dream highway with your Queen behind the steering wheel, saying, "Hey, big dream, I'm coming for you!" And you start to see the guy who's not ready as a little detour, and just say, "Thanks for the lessons. You were really, really close, but you weren't it."

Doing this takes courage, certainty and belief in yourself.

But if you don't embody your Queen essence and the magic of who you truly are, how do you expect a man to treat you like a Queen and love you for you?

There's real freedom in being able to have tough conversations and being confident in who you are. There's power in knowing that what you have is so special that you don't need to ever overcompensate again. You don't need to wait for someone to be ready EVER again.

Doesn't that feel amazing?

One final point I want to be clear on here: I'm not saying that if a guy doesn't want to marry you after a single date then... bye! That's a little intense - and I guarantee it doesn't come from your powerful Queen self.
What I am saying is that when you get to those natural moments of uncertainty in a relationship, be brave, be vulnerable and come from your Queen self. Otherwise, you'll spend your life holding out for the guy to be ready.

That's just being in love with someone's potential, and it's a complete waste of time. That 'potential' may not ever be realized in this lifetime. When you wait around for it, you put your dreams on hold. You put your fertility on hold. You betray everything that you desire.

Are you going to do that for the sake of some guy who's not ready? Fuck no, not anymore, Queen!

VULNERABILITY IS AN INSIDE JOB

Look at your life right now and get honest with yourself. This is an opportunity for you to redefine what vulnerability will be for you from now on. Because you've got to look clearly at what is, and how you've been operating and relating to vulnerability, to understand what it looks like from a place of power.

That's what Queens do.

If you've never seen a Queen, just think of someone like Beyoncé, or a friend who has a fricking amazing relationship. Start to break down and identify what it is about this woman's essence that sets her apart. You'll find she has a deep belief in herself and a presence of enough-ness, and she stands fully in who she is.

Queens expect love to work out. They allow their men to see the fullness of themselves. And, as we've talked about above, that's what vulnerability is. It's letting men see who you genuinely are, warts and all.

Honestly, when I let vulnerability into my life and tried it on - when I was willing to actually let people and audiences feel me - it was life-changing. I started to book amazing auditions and incredible roles. That was when things started to totally change in my acting career.

The change also expanded out into my personal life. I noticed it in my friendships and in my relationship with my mum and my brother. And of course, I noticed it with the type of men that I was attracting in. Everything massively up-leveled, and it felt so different and fucking amazing.

Now, please hear me: my vulnerability was a brand-new muscle, so I was definitely finding my way. But I liked what I was noticing. And I wondered, *"Wow, how did I not know this? How was I trying to do relationships before without letting myself be seen?"* Once I gave myself permission to let people in to see who I truly was, I discovered that that's what creates true intimacy. And then, when I did my daily mindset work to get intimate with myself, and spent time in my Vortex creating my reality? That's when it all took off.

Let's briefly talk about true intimacy. I've often seen the word broken down into 'in-to-me-I-see', which I love. There's the golden nugget: the first person that you need to be intimate with is yourself. You need to be able to see and love and cherish the amazing woman that you are before you can expect anyone else to be able to do that too. And you need to know and love your body, so you can turn yourself on! There's no shortcut.

When it comes to relating to someone else, there's a huge freaking difference between sex and intimacy. Anyone can have sex, but bringing intimacy into your sex life is a whole other level. And the truth is that intimacy is about letting the other person see you. It's about being with that person emotionally, not just physically. It's allowing your full expression to show up in the bedroom, and asking for what you want instead of over-giving and turning into a sex barbie who just wants to make the man happy.

Meanwhile, by not being vulnerable, you're compartmentalizing who you are. You're just giving people these tiny little snippets of yourself. You're not showing up for yourself or letting people in. And that's incredibly stingy, because why the hell would you live that small version of yourself?

It's inauthentic, and it's fucking mediocre.

Not only that, but not bringing in your heart and not sharing your flaws and insecurities and fears with people is exactly why you can't make it past the third date (or whenever your personal saboteurs show up). It's why you attract in emotionally unavailable men, and why relationships aren't working for you. This is why you might be in a relationship today, but it's not one that's connected. It's not intimate. It's not supportive. So really, darling, why bother?

That all happens because - and I know you know this by now, beauty, but it bears repeating - you're not in a soulmate relationship with the most important person in your life: YOU.

Some of you have never been in a soulmate relationship. That's okay, but isn't it about time you let yourself have that?
Fully let this sink in for you. It might feel confronting. It might feel scary. It might even feel exhilarating the way it did for me.
You might feel all sorts of emotions coming up at the moment, and that's perfect. Remember: Rome wasn't built in a day.

Still though, try to let even just a fraction of this conversation in. Just sit with it for a breath or two, and get that this doesn't need to be the way that you live for one more minute. Get that you CAN choose yourself. Get that the only way into a soulmate relationship is by giving yourself permission to let people genuinely see you. And get that this means first, YOU have to see you - and that it's unsafe to keep your heart closed.

Bit by bit, let yourself take that in. It's not only safe, but it's also vital to keep your heart open if you want to live a lit-up life. If you want to thrive in this life, that's the deal.

QUEENS DON'T GRIND

One way that you can refuse to let yourself be vulnerable is by not honoring your needs. Knowing your needs - coming from your heart and respecting them - is an important part of connecting with your vulnerability.

So many women come to me living 100% from their masculine: that 'do, do, do' paradigm we talked about in depth in Chapter 9. That's no surprise - it's exactly where I used to live from.
This mentality usually carries fight-or-flight, 'make it happen' energy. It often feels good for a while, because there's an adrenaline buzz that keeps the energy alive. But leading with your masculine long-term does more than just deplete your adrenals along the way. It also depletes your soul, because there's no flow, ease or grace in this paradigm.

Flow, ease, grace and trust are feminine traits. Allowing them to govern and lead the way sets you up for an entirely different life. It's expansive with no hustle, and it requires a lot less effort. Just let yourself feel that... feels so good, right?

In this paradigm, you don't need to prove anything. You don't need to push or take action simply for the sake of getting closer to your goal. Instead, you take inspired action from a place that feels good and from a deeper knowing.

Living in the masculine paradigm wore me out to my core. That's how I know that it feels like shit for you. It stems from lack and a poverty-consciousness mindset. It stems from not trusting life. Deep down, you don't trust that things can work out for you unless you work really, really hard to get them.

And, quite frankly, that's exhausting and fucking unsustainable.

RESTING AND RECEIVING IS A PROCESS

*I recently caught myself grinding to meet deadlines. I was
a new mum, and I was exhausted. I sat down to do some
editing on this book one night, and I was like, "I just CAN"T
right now." I felt my heart whispering, "Lucy, you need to
fucking slow down."*

*So I shut down my computer, emailed my editors and told them
I was taking ten days off from my business, and if we need
to shift the book's timeline then so be it. I needed rest and I
needed to get back to my joy, lightness, ease and flow.*

*It was such a huge moment for me, because I have so much
energy and I love what I do so much that the lines can easily
blur. Then, just after I'd declared my ten days of rest to my
husband, we ended up having a huge, whopping disagreement.
That might sound bad, but let me tell you, we NEEDED that to
happen. Things we were both ignoring suddenly had room to
breathe, and they came up thick and fast.*

*The disagreement was uncomfortable at the time (because we
don't disagree much at all), but it cleared the decks for us to set
up our life even more intentionally. It meant I could rest and
be super-present for both myself and my family.*

*I clicked back into abundance, and we went on to have a record
month in my business. Isn't that rad? That's what can show up
when you make a sacred vow to stop grinding and get in flow
with the Divine.*

The thing is that most of us aren't taught to rest. I know I wasn't. I seriously used to work myself into the ground. I'd only rest if I was too bone-tired to physically work anymore. WTF?! This is SO messed up. And if you're living like this right now, then sister, I'm inviting you to give up this shitty way of living for good.

GRINDING IS MASCULINE. RESTING IS FEMININE.

I've already told you how epic my mum is. Honestly, I don't know where she gets all her energy from! BUT... she just doesn't know how to spell rest. Yes, she gets early nights, so that's definitely something... but she's also a typical Aries with that masculine energy of 'go, go, go, do, do, do!'

My brother and I used to joke growing up that every weekend, all we wanted to do was sleep in and take it easy. Meanwhile, Mum would say, "You guys are so lazy! I have jobs for you. Now get up and let's get cracking!" Even if we went on vacation, my mum just couldn't sit still. She's so hardwired to be of service and get things done because doing them makes her feel productive.

But, at a deeper level, 'doing' also makes her feel worthy. She's a big believer that you have to work hard to do well. And I inherited that belief system from her, so I had to put a lot of effort into divorcing it.

I love my mum to bits and we're very close, so this isn't a dig at her. I just wanted to share my story with you to remind you that these beliefs get passed down through generations. There's no surprise about where I picked up this way of being, and I invite you to look at where you may have inherited it from.

If it's going to stop, it needs to stop with you. And it needs to stop right now.

I know I don't want my kids living out of this 'work, work, work' paradigm, so I made sure it stopped with me. It's still something I'm working on, and I know I can slip back into it if I go into autopilot. But whenever that happens, I'm pretty quick to pull myself up and stop it in its tracks.

REST IS YOUR BIRTHRIGHT

You deserve rest. It's your freaking birthright.

Rest nourishes your mind, body and soul. Resting is a way of putting your deep trust in the Universe and knowing that you're never working alone. Going into grind and hustle mode closes down your connection. It slams your heart shut.

When you make rest non-negotiable, you'll find you become WAYYYY more productive with whatever you need to get done. Slowing down actually speeds up your productivity, because after you've rested, you're working from grace. It feels effortless and fun and in flow.

Can you feel the difference? So lush, isn't it?

I also want to be clear that when I talk about 'rest', I don't mean staying in bed and sleeping all day. That kind of 'rest' is a sign that you're probably avoiding something, and possibly, that you're depressed.

The rest I'm talking about is intentional, and is just a part of your day. It might be taking a 30-minute catnap in the early afternoon. Or maybe it's giving yourself the gift of a few super-early nights.

Whatever it is though, think of it as being just as non-negotiable as a meeting with your boss. This is critical for you to step into your inner Queen. Why?

Queens don't grind. They're in flow with the Divine.

Taking a rest is THE biggest act of self-love and self-care you can do for yourself. There's a reason that one of the most common forms of torture is sleep deprivation. Sleep deficits are part of why we have so much anxiety in the world. They exist because we've been programmed to grind and pull all-nighters like it's something to be proud of.

But nothing could be further from the truth. Prioritizing yourself by getting your rest is sexy! It's your way of saying, "I love myself and I fucking matter!" to the Universe. It plugs you into your deserve-ability in a massive way, and cultivates a healthy, loving relationship with yourself all the way down to your cells.

PRIORITIZING REST AND PLEASURE SUPERCHARGES YOU

Priya came to me hardwired to over-give, people-please and consistently put herself second. She used to regularly pull all-nighters for her job, and she was so in her head that I almost canceled our call after connecting with her. I honestly didn't think she was ready to do the work.

So I handed her a massive dose of truth. I told her that if she wanted to continue with the call, I needed her to get into her heart right then and there.

When she heard that, she immediately burst into tears. She saw how shut-down and numb she'd become. She admitted to me in that moment that she was borderline depressed, and that she was so sick of feeling left behind and like no man wanted her.

Priya knew she could easily have an arranged marriage, but she didn't want to go down that path, even if it meant being alone.

She wanted intimacy. She wanted connection with someone she loved. And more than anything, she wanted to be a mum. I felt for her so much. I could feel her heart crying out. But I knew amongst all that misery, her inner Queen was busting to come out.

Priya had to work through a LOT of long-repressed feelings. She uncovered a need to prove to her mum that she was enough, and realized she still had to deal with abandonment issues from her dad. She also had to nurture her inner little girl and completely crack open that independent archetype she was working from.

But once she finally surrendered to the process and got vulnerable, she could see how much she was living in her head. She truly got how disconnected she'd become from her body, soul and sensuality, and it woke her up big-time. I remember her saying halfway through the program, "Lucy you haven't seen anything yet! I'm going to blow your mind by Week 8."

And do you know what? She was right.

Watching her metamorphosis was magical. She focused on opening her heart and living vulnerably from her place of feminine power. She prioritized rest, joy and creating from her Vortex. The change was palpable. All her fellow Queens in the program kept telling her how magnetic her new energy was, how soft and present she was and how deeply it inspired them.

For the first time in her life, Priya felt seen, understood, held and important. She felt worthy for just being herself – not for what she did in her career. She started prioritizing pleasure enough to give herself daily orgasms, and she was like a wild woman unleashed.

So much shifted for her because she began to put rest and pleasure first, and her to-do list came second. Obviously, she used other elements in my process too, but for Priya, resting was the key to getting into her heart.

Divine woman, I am so bloody excited for you to take this on and make it non-negotiable. Trust me: if I can thrive as an Aussie girl who used to be a 2am-pulling grind machine, running herself into the ground with anxiety up to her eyeballs, then you can change too! It's the only way to live if you want to feel peaceful in your soul and live an abundant, rich, happy, healthy life.

As a reminder, here are your Queen identity traits:

- Rest.
- Relaxation.
- Allowing.
- Trust.
- Receiving.
- Joy.
- Fun.
- Pleasure.

As I've said before, walking around with a closed heart never serves you. Think of where you are today because of how you've been operating. How much has it cost you already? Your joy? Stress? Anxiety? Illness? Constant worry? Shame? Maybe you've put your fertility on the line.

Beauty, that's the huge cost of only just getting through your life and trying to do relationships with your heart closed. It's time to open your heart and trust the process - and that's where we're going in the next chapter.

THE GOLD NUGGETS

Beautiful woman, we've covered some gold together in the last few pages. Here's a quick recap of the 24-karat nuggets to take away with you and treasure as you head into the next chapter:

- There's a fricking HUGE difference between vulnerability and neediness.

- Vulnerability means standing in your feminine power, being honest about what you want, and being prepared to 'bless and release' if someone's not on board with it.

- Neediness, on the other hand, is about giving all your power away to the other person and letting them decide what's going to happen.

- Being vulnerable is 100% an inside job - it requires getting intimate with yourself before you can get intimate with anyone else.

- The key is to keep your heart open - so if you like someone who's not right for you, your heart stays open enough to meet someone who is.

GIFT WORK

Over to you, superstar! Let's get vulnerable and practice what it feels like so you can change your entire world!

First up, I've recorded a meditation for you. Head on over to _www.soultosoulglobal.com/book-bonuses_ to find it and listen. Commit to listening to it as many times each day as necessary to really FEEL your vulnerability.

Next, journal your answers to these questions and notice the sensations in your body as you do. What emotions come up?

- Honestly, how much of yourself do you bring to dating / relationships? Give yourself a score from 1-10.
- What holds you back from being all of who you are?
- Do you ask for what you truly want in relationships, or is it more important for you to be liked and to please the other person?
- Where do you hold back with expressing what you want? FEEL into why you do this. What fears do you have around speaking up and asking for what you want?
- Have you ever experienced true intimacy? If so, describe it.

Now, explore your feelings about resting and receiving.

- Whose story have you inherited that tells you that you have to work hard to do well? Maybe you believe you have to work hard for love, or that you have to work yourself into the ground to be successful and earn money.

- Why do you find it hard to rest just for the sake of it, and not because you're sick or run down?

- What do you think will happen if you let yourself rest? Does anxiety come up when you imagine yourself making rest a part of your daily routine, or do you feel yourself relaxing internally and being able to breathe a little deeper?

- Write a new story right now about your Queen self who rests daily. How does she feel about herself? How does she feel in her body? How does she feel about the world? How does she feel about love?

Finally, record the following mantra on your phone and listen to it constantly:

"Rest is my birthright. I am held by the Divine in every moment. I thrive because I rest. I am an expert at resting and receiving. I am divine, abundant, radiant and enough. I am a Queen. My world expands effortlessly when I rest."

CHAPTER TWELVE

Don't Judge

YOUR PROCESS

"Comparing yourself to other people is toxic. Celebrating another person's victory is like saying to the Universe, "I'm ready to receive that and more."

I've said it before in this book, darling one, but it's worth repeating: transformation is a process. It might look like a long process, or it might appear - from the outside - to happen overnight. But either way, it's vital to honor that process, be your own cheerleader and just go with wherever it leads you.

More than that, transformation is YOUR sacred process. It's not a one-size-fits-all PDF document that you can just download. It works differently for everyone, and it can generate different results for each person. Those results all come down to how committed you are and how much you're willing to trust your process.

Of course, 'trusting in the process' can be super-challenging when you're right in the middle of it. So in this chapter, I want to cover some of the triggers that probably came up as you were reading this book. And then I want to give you some tools to help you get to the other side of them, so you can see real transformation unfolding in your life.

TRANSFORMATION IS AN INDIVIDUAL PROCESS

The process of transformation is unique to everyone. If you and your bestie read these pages together, I can almost guarantee that you'll have totally individual experiences with them.

She'll read one chapter and have a dramatic, hellz-to-the-fucking-YES breakthrough with it. Meanwhile, you'll be reading the same thing with your forehead scrunched up, thinking, *"WTF is this Lucy chick on about here?"* Then, maybe later she'll find herself bawling her eyes out because she's massively triggered by a particular chapter. When you read it though, you'll just nod and say, "Well, duh. Yeah, of course - THAT's not news to me."

There's nothing wrong with either reaction. Neither of you should be doing anything differently. It's just that you've each got your own processes and your own stuff to work through. And as long as you're both willing to trust in and stay with your own process, you'll each get the transformation you're looking for.

I'm rooting for you to become the badass rockstar at relationships that you were born to be. I'm rooting for you to ignite that Queen living inside of you who knows how to create her best life. So I'm going to keep it as real as I possibly can for you. The world NEEDS your brilliance, your light and your bigness more than ever right now. That's why I want to take care of any hiccups that might stop you from making yourself your No. 1 priority. Because remember: until you make yourself your biggest priority, no one else will.

> *Once again, until it's about you, it's never going to be about you.*

WHAT DOES 'TRUSTING YOUR PROCESS' REALLY MEAN?

In a nutshell, trusting your process means giving up your expectations and attachments to the outcome you want to create, eg. attracting your soulmate or anything else. It means being fluid with the process. Imagine your process as a river that you're floating downstream on. There are going to be currents, the odd branch and a few rocks that will catch you off-guard in the river. Usually, they'll take the form of uncomfortable emotions that you haven't felt in a very long time, or resentments and anger from your deeper self that you've been ignoring. And you're going to want to resist those currents. You're going to want to resist them so hard.

But if you fight against them, you'll start to feel like they're dragging you under. The truth is that they HAVE been dragging you under until this very moment. And it's been taking all your energy to push back against them.

That's why you constantly feel exhausted.

So instead of resisting that current to struggle back upstream to where your old BS story and limitations live, you need to learn to flow with it. You need to let those emotions flow through you. And that means letting the floodgates open and honoring whatever comes through them. Feel everything fully, the way we talked about in Chapter 6, and then release it.

Let all the shit come to the surface... And then, once you've released it, you get to connect deeply with all the epic dreams you've buried so far down that you forgot you even had them.

A word of caution: you can only flow with and honor what comes up if you set aside time and space for it to emerge. That means you need to prioritize time to sit with this book and simply let yourself be with its content. Then prioritize the work you find yourself needing to do after reading. That might be journaling. It might be the Rage Pages you learned about in Chapter 8. It might be having a big ol' ugly cry. Or it could be all three together.

Don't try to fit the chapters that feel super-vulnerable and tender for you into a 15-minute morning interval on a day when you have a lot of other plans. Put yourself first and take a solid chunk of time out for YOU to honor whatever your process requires.
You wouldn't put off an important meeting with your CEO, would you? You don't get to put off this important meeting with yourself either, got it? This is where you're going to ramp up your self-worth by prioritizing yourself, dealing with your shit and doing whatever it takes to get that magnificent heart of yours open.

"But Lucy, how much time will this take?" I hear you ask. And seriously, I can't answer that for you - how long is a piece of string? All I can tell you is that you shouldn't feel rushed or like you have to stop abruptly and suddenly switch gears to get to your next appointment of the day. You'll know within yourself when something feels complete. You'll know once you've felt everything that's there to feel in the moment.

Now's the time to hang up your masculine hat (if you haven't already) and plug into your divine feminine. Remember in the last chapter, we talked all about vulnerability and how to come from a place of divine feminine power? Remember how we talked about 'flowing and feeling' being the feminine, while 'pushing and making things happen' is masculine? Can you feel the difference, beauty? The heart energy is feminine, while overthinking and ticking things off is masculine.

But I guarantee that if you get in the way of your process by staying too busy for it (which is being too busy for yourself), nothing will change. And these pages, which could give you the keys to the kingdom of everything you want, will instead end up being just another book you read once.

RESISTANCE CAN LOOK DIFFERENT FOR EVERYONE

It's probably important to mention that - just as the process can look different for everyone - so can the response of resisting it. For example, resistance to what's coming up as you read this book might look like:

- **Not being able to believe in yourself**: it could mean seeing yourself as 'damaged goods' or some kind of lost cause that this stuff could never work for.

  If this is you, I want you to trash that shitty story this instant. You, divine woman, are not broken. We're not fixing anything here. You're just shining a light on all those stories, insecurities and wounds that are currently working against you. Then you can let them go and replace them with epic new stories that you're excited to live into.

- **Getting angry** - or at least annoyed - with me: it's totally normal for human beings to externalize any resistance we feel and blame whoever 'made' us realize that it's there. The good news is that if you find yourself rolling your eyes hard enough to strain

TWELVE | Don't Judge **YOUR PROCESS**

something at any point as you read, it's a flashing neon sign that there's something to uncover.

If this is you, lean into the resistance, open yourself up to it and see what lessons and messages it has for you.

(Incidentally... you might think you're just 'a bit annoyed' with something you read in here. But I can almost guarantee that if you dig down into that 'annoyance', you're going to find it's a thin, sociably acceptable veneer of irritation over a giant, roiling pool of rage. And if so, celebrate it. Because when you connect with that rage, it's going to be super-fucking-powerful!)

- **Feeling impatient** (this is a big one): maybe you'll find yourself in the middle of a chapter and suddenly realize that you're itching to get to the end of it. Or maybe you'll catch yourself thinking, "Lucy, just get on with it, already!" If so, there's almost certainly something in that chapter you just don't want to acknowledge.

Again, if this is you, you need to trust in your process. And that means leaning in and feeling into whatever's causing your resistance to being with the current chapter.

DEALING WITH RESISTANCE

Noticing any resistance you have is the first step. But what do you do with it once you've identified it?

I started to talk about the answer to this question in the bullet points above. However, I might have been getting ahead of myself a little, because the most important thing you need to know is that when you notice resistance, you're going to want to judge it.

Trust me on this. As soon as you bite the bullet and acknowledge that, yep, that right there is a seething whirlpool of resistance, you'll look for someone or something to blame. It's very tempting, I know. But you already know that when you blame, you give your power away. When you own your resistance - lean into it and embrace it - you supercharge your power.

Often, the someone you want to blame is yourself. You might find yourself feeling like you 'shouldn't' be feeling this resistance. Or maybe you feel that you're doing something wrong - that you should 'know better' than this, or that you 'should have dealt with this shit ten years ago'. Maybe you'll feel like you've done so much work already that any resistance you identify should magically combust like a vampire the moment sunlight touches it.

(And look, yes, sometimes - especially after you've been working with this process for a while - that will absolutely happen. But even the most evolved of us still get resistance coming up. We just get good at pivoting and embracing it, instead of letting it frustrate us.)

Other times, you might find yourself wanting to blame someone else for your resistance. It might be me, since I'm the one who's pushing you to look at it. But it might equally be someone involved in the situation that created your resistance - or even the situation itself.

You might find yourself saying, "Well yeah, of course I'm experiencing resistance - and I'd be able to let it go the way I'm meant to if it wasn't for [fill in the blank]." The problem, sister, is that means you're blaming whatever you filled in the blank with, and then 'it' has all the power. I'm pretty sure you don't want that - because that's what's keeping you in Victim Village, where the coffee sucks and the people are douche-y!

Regardless of who or what you blame, the fact that there's blame going on is a crystal-clear sign that you're also judging. And that, beautiful woman, can be an issue - although, for God's sake, please don't start judging yourself for the judging. It's so easy to get bogged down and stuck in all that judgment. But as you learned in Chapter 3, like everything else in your life, it's a choice. For example:

- You can choose at any time to step back from that resistance - to simply accept that it's there and that it has an important message for you.
- You can become the observer and imagine looking down at it from a distance, as though you're an eagle soaring through the sky and

seeing your resistance from a higher perspective.

· You can choose to have immense compassion and love for the 'you' who's trying so hard to protect herself by creating that resistance.

· You can choose to be curious about it, fascinated by it and grateful for the chance to really uncover what's going on and do something with it.

Or, of course, you can choose to stay stuck and bogged down where you are right now. You can get angry and frustrated with whoever or whatever you're blaming and continue to play the victim.

But you can guess which of those options can change your life and help you grasp the valuable lessons with more juicy ease, right?

Get excited when you discover the rage

Look, I get it - it feels incredibly shitty when you first connect with that turbulent ball of rage that's bubbling away deep under the surface. Remember: no matter HOW perfect our childhoods were, we all have that rage. It's the remnants of all the things that we didn't want to happen. The things that were too heavy and hard to feel at the time, and that we didn't have the support to deal with or even give ourselves permission to feel.

Instead, we listened to the voices of everyone around us who told us, "Just suck it up. You'll get over it. You'll be fine." But you know what? We didn't get over it. Not truly. We just pushed it down where we didn't have to deal with it anymore, and it's still just as fucking alive as it's ever been.

That 'pushing it down' hasn't served you, sister. The fact that you're reading this book now to help you change your life is clear proof that it hasn't served you one bit.

That was exactly where I was too until I dealt with the rage deep inside me. I've been where you're standing and it's seriously uncomfortable. But nothing good ever happens inside our comfort zones, so it's time to get messy and let it all come up and out.

It's toxic for that rage to live another day inside of you. If I can transform my rage into power, I know you can too. In fact, the Soul to Soul module on rage is one of my clients' favorites, because they feel so free and liberated after they commit to it. Some of my clients even call the Rage Pages exercise their 'Power Pages'!

And yes, it's going to take grit and commitment to prioritize the time and space to sit with your rage - to explore it, look it square in the face and lean into it 100%. I get that. But I promise you, it'll be SO worth it. On the other hand, if you put it off or make excuses, you're essentially just putting yourself off and making excuses to stay safe so nothing will change.

You may discover that you have a hard, thick shell of numbness that's built over the top of your rage, which you need to crack through first. If so, all you have to do, my darling, is commit to the process. My clients have stuff like this coming all the time, and yes, they sometimes want to skip this part. But once they commit, they have huge breakthroughs to the point that some of them go back and revisit the process to dig even deeper.

So keep letting yourself be with whatever's there - even if it doesn't seem to be anything huge or dramatic at first. Keep digging, baby! You can do this.

I promise you that one day, you'll wake up and say something like, "Oh my God! I didn't realize just how numb I was. I wonder what's sitting there under the numbness?" Or it might be, "Oh, wow. I think I might be starting to feel just a tiny bit more today than I managed yesterday!" Either way, those are HUGE wins and definitely things to celebrate.

They might look like tiny achievements on the surface, but beauty, I want you to know that they're big breakthroughs. So celebrate them, because they're a sign that you're on the right path. Write them into your journal and get excited about them.

> *When we celebrate the small*
> *wins, they turn into big wins.*

Oh, and like I said in Chapter 8, when you connect with your inner rage, celebrate the fuck out of that too. You don't need to feel one ounce of shame around it.

In fact, feeling guilty or ashamed of rage - or anything else, for that matter - is toxic. Pushing your rage down and repressing it because of that shame is a toxic double-whammy that will make you physically sick if you keep doing it.

Shame is a useless emotion that only keeps you in a holding pattern of stuckness. It's time to spread those wings, expand and be unapologetic with your self-expression. When you connect with your rage - when you can pull it up from the depths of where you've been hiding it - you'll free yourself.

And if you're wondering exactly how to do that, don't worry. I've got you, girl! I've created a meditation to help, plus the 'Rage Pages' exercise in Chapter 8 will get you nailing your rage like a pro.

This is one of the most potent gifts you can give yourself, so make time to put your ALL into this. Don't cut corners. Don't be half-assed. Commit to it like the rockstar that you are.

OPPORTUNITIES TO BUILD YOUR
TRUST MUSCLE ARE EVERYWHERE

An acting class exercise gave me one of the most amazing chances to honor my process that I can remember experiencing.

In the exercise, we had to pretend to make a phone call. This involved dropping into our hearts and acting out the call as if it were a real conversation we needed to have with one of our parents. We could choose whichever parent we felt we harbored the most anger, hurt or abandonment toward. And I realized that the conversation I needed to have (and have in front of all my classmates) was with my dad.

At first, I felt huge resistance around the idea. I was terrified of tapping into this part of me, in case my emotions were too strong for me to handle. So I was like, "Holy fuck, I'm NOT doing this ridiculous exercise. I mean, my dad is dead!"

(Remember that I still missed my dad like crazy as an adult. So the idea of saying anything bad about him – let alone tearing strips off him in public – felt like a huge betrayal of his memory. In fact, I didn't think I was angry with him at all. I thought I was just sad – but how wrong I was! My resistance was an outward reflection of how apologetic I felt about having these 'bad', 'unacceptable' feelings that I really didn't want to consciously acknowledge.)

I watched a classmate do the exercise, and it was so fricking REAL that I almost heard her mum on the other end of the call with her. It was palpable and powerful, and I shrank into my chair, wondering how the hell I'd be able to connect at that level.

So when it was my turn, I tried to reach out for the rage that I sensed was there — and that my mentor had known I was feeling — but I couldn't quite manage it. I was just too soft, and I kept making all these excuses for him as a way of denying my little girl her right to her rage.

I did the same thing on Try #2. But then, on my third try, something just clicked for me. I fully unleashed, and it felt fucking amazing. I gave myself permission to let go and genuinely go there, and then I let it rip like a woman on a mission.

I finally connected smack-bang-HARD with a deep rage that I'd never even known existed — and everyone in that room was mesmerized by my connection to my truth. I accessed my self-expression for the first time in its rawest, grittiest form. I 'talked to my dad' through the class exercise, and just fucking let him have it. I swore at him like a trooper — no holding back and no being the 'nice girl' I'd trained myself to be for so long.

I was so in the moment that time felt like it stopped. I'll never forget it.

Then finally, when all the rage had erupted out of me and there was nothing else left, I finished with, "Dad, I love you." And believe me when I tell you that my Universe tilted on its axis that day. Something shifted and ignited deep inside me. It was like nothing in my world would ever be the same again.

I felt light and supercharged — like I'd just scraped away layers and layers of repressed, unfelt emotion. I felt as though I'd just had a taste of my true voice, my true power, and all I could think was, "YES! More, please!"

My classmates never saw me the same way again, and neither did I.

I guarantee that I wouldn't be married to the love of my life today – or be a mum in such a healthy, loving, secure relationship – if I hadn't dealt with my scared, stifled, repressed, eight-year-old self in that exercise.

And I've seen the same thing happen for so many of the women doing this work with me. Sometimes, the person at the heart of their rage is a parent who's still alive. Sometimes it's an ex-boyfriend – and sometimes, that ex has written a totally unprompted apology with no idea that my client did the rage work the previous day.

It's yet more proof that we're all energy and all connected, even if we don't realize it.

It's important to be aware that connecting with your rage isn't a 'one-and-done' kind of exercise. You'll constantly discover new aspects and elements of it over time. It'll pop up in the strangest of places. But each time you connect with it and let it go, the process will get easier and less uncomfortable.

In fact, you may not feel like it right now, but - like the clients I mentioned earlier - this is going to become one of your favorite tools. It's going to serve you big-time. You'll feel like you have a secret, go-to trick up your sleeve for whenever you experience the anger and rage that often hide under frustration.

Eventually, you'll get to the point where you're standing in a queue to get coffee, suddenly notice something's triggered your rage, and you'll know exactly how to deal with it. So you'll get to the front of the line, place your cappuccino order, go outside while the barista makes it and deal with your rage in the moment.

You'll be able to step back to get curious about what's truly coming up for you. You'll be able to ask yourself deeper questions like, "What is this actually about?" and, "What's underneath my trigger?" Then you'll be able to put your hands on your heart and close your eyes to re-center and ground yourself.

Later on, at home, you can do some Rage Pages on the trigger to dissolve it once and for all. But right then and there, you can get clear on what the rage is truly about. Then you can choose to pivot like a rockstar and move forward powerfully with your day.
So by the time your coffee's ready, you'll at least have shifted the energy, neutralized the charge and gotten it out of your immediate Vortex.

The key is not to fight against or resist that rage.

Let yourself feel your rage. Then transmute it, and finally release it. When you can do that, your rage becomes full-blown creatrix energy, and you can use it to bring anything you want into your Vortex.
Let your rage take up all the fucking space darling. It's yours... all of it!

THIS BOOK CAN'T TRANSFORM YOU

Brace yourself, beauty, because I have another truthbomb for you. We started talking about the dangers of intellectual self-development back in Chapter 5, but it's time to revisit that idea again now. Why? Because there's no way this book can give you the medicine you need to bring in your soulmate and transform your life without YOUR cooperation, co-creation and commitment.

If you really want to milk the shit out of this book and get the breakthroughs you've been starving for, you're going to NEED to prioritize the work in it. Just like I did, you're going to need to block out time in your calendar to do the exercises. Then you'll need to sit your beautiful ass down with your journal and connect with yourself, your emotions and your dreams.

You don't want to rush or force anything, but you also don't want to stifle any breakthroughs by not giving them space to happen in.

And, coming full circle to the topic of the chapter, the only way you can pull THAT off is to cultivate a deep reverence for your process, however it unfolds. When stuff comes up - and it will eventually if you let it - you need to prepare to get seriously gritty, roll up your sleeves and face it head-on.

YOU CAN'T RUSH THE PROCESS

Annie is a British client who's in my Soul to Soul group. Her uncle had sexually abused her when she was just five years old. Plus, her mother had been super-tough on her, telling her that, "In our house, we don't sit around crying. We just stand up and keep going, because we're strong."

So Annie had totally numbed out. She'd always kept the abuse secret, sure that her mother couldn't carry that burden on top of everything else.

It wasn't until she started working with me and discovered the Rage Pages exercise that anything shifted for Annie. She resisted trying the exercise at first — sure that it would open up Pandora's box, and that what she found would be too full-on for her to handle. Plus, when she first came to see me, she was super-impatient. She just wanted to tick the boxes and get things done.

I told her that it didn't work that way, and that she couldn't rush her process. She needed to prioritize spending time on this work, and allow whatever came up for her to come up instead of trying to control it.

So she summoned up her courage and committed to dedicating time to her Rage Pages. And much to her surprise, she LOVED the exercise. She was in awe of how freeing it was to give her little girl the voice she needed to express all that deep-down rage and resentment. She cleared all her feelings of unworthiness and being a damaged human being, and stepped into her true, powerful, beautiful self. And now she literally can't get enough of doing Rage Pages. They make her feel like the woman she was born to be has finally come out into the world.

All her fellow Soul to Soul Queens are stunned at how different Annie is now too. One woman told her she looked, "ten times lighter". Not only that, but she'd always seemed a bit harsh before you got to know her... and suddenly, she seemed much softer and more available.

Of course, Annie's loving her new magnetism and can't wait to attract her soulmate from this place.

The magic, the transformation and the enormous breakthroughs are all here for the taking. You've just got to be 100% in the process, and genuinely willing to get results.

Congratulations on backing yourself this far!

We've talked before about just how essential it is to back yourself, because there's nobody else who can do it for you. Yes, good friends or mentors can help you to realize that you're worth backing - but you're the only one who can truly back yourself.

So I want to give you a massive high-five, right here and now. Just the fact that you've got this far in the book means you've deeply honored yourself. You've stuck with it - read each chapter, and hopefully, done most of the gift work too. That means you're giving yourself true self-love.

If you haven't done any gift work yet, check in with yourself. Ask yourself what your excuses are... then stop making them, dive in and get started right now. Here's a clue: the excuse you're using to justify not doing the gift work is exactly the same one you use to justify love never working out for you. You don't believe it will work for you if you give it everything you've got, so you hold back.

One final truthbomb for this chapter, sister. You're either going to slap this belief in the face, show it who's boss and get to work, or you're going to be single this time next year and do sweet fuck all.

Choose.

If you've been prioritizing yourself and doing the work this far, you deserve to take a bright red lipstick and write "I am a fucking ROCKSTAR!" across your bedroom mirror. Seriously - go out today, buy yourself a bunch of flowers and write yourself a love letter that celebrates the shit out of how far you've come.

But please, divine woman, once you've done all those things, do NOT stop.
You've come too far to give up now.

Your future isn't written yet, and it's the things you do now that will help you to write it. Again, you're the only one who can write that story - so make sure that when you do, you only put the things you want in it. Do not play small. Do not settle.

And do NOT be apologetic about any of it.

THE GOLD NUGGETS

Beautiful woman, we've covered some gold together in the last few pages. Here's a quick recap of the 24-karat nuggets to take away with you and treasure as you head into the next chapter:

- Transformation isn't an instant download from the Universe - it's a process.

- It's often an incredibly uncomfortable process, so you might be tempted to avoid it (and you can do that in a few different ways).

- However, the gold only happens in your life if you stop avoiding resistance, and instead commit full-out to prioritizing your process every day.

- So be brave, put yourself and this work first and above all, TRUST IN YOUR PROCESS.

GIFT WORK

Over to you, superstar! This is such a juicy gift work section that I can't wait for you to get into it.

First, dig into your Rage Pages. It's time again to make a space to get down and dirty with your rage. If you didn't go there when I introduced you to Rage Pages in Chapter 8, I want you to do it now. Block out time for them this week, and KEEP that time as sacred in your calendar. I encourage you to do them in the evening when you have time to really tune in to your body and be fully present.

If you need a reminder of how exactly to do your Rage Pages, check out the Gift work section in Chapter 8. And remember that Rage Pages aren't a one-off thing. You'll need to make time to do them over and over, to keep clearing the shit from your past and create a sparkling future.

Next, darling woman, if you feel off-track, and find yourself shrinking from facing your rage, remind yourself to keep going! Keep in mind that it took me three goes to fully get into it. But if you feel blocked - and it happens to all of us sometimes - go to _www.soultosoulglobal. com/book-bonuses_ and listen to the SOS meditation I've created just for this situation. Get yourself back on track so you can shine!

Finally, here's something that's great to do once you've finished your Rage Pages for the evening. I want you to tap into your little girl and write a story that excites the fuck out of you down on paper. Envision your ideal life and create it! Then stick your story on your bedside table and regularly read it to yourself out loud.

I like to write a letter to the Universe, thanking it for bringing me all the things that I want. I have so much fun while I write this. Whatever you write, feel your dream life into existence ... feed that into your Vortex, and then watch the magic start to manifest.

CHAPTER THIRTEEN

Be

UNAPOLOGETIC

"I give zero fucks what anyone thinks.
I only care what I think."

Let's be real: most women today are stuck in the habit of living apologetic lives because they're terrified of judgment. Some deep-down part of them is freaking out from the fear of being burned at the stake if they speak their truth... so instead, they hold back.

The problem, darling one, is that that keeps them small. It keeps them trapped in tiny little boxes that they make for themselves and then hold themselves prisoner in. Those boxes might look like waiting for permission, waiting to be saved or just giving up and settling.

But you deserve SO MUCH more than any of those. You deserve to feel purpose, freedom and joy. So in this chapter, we'll talk about how to claim that life for yourself - totally, utterly and 100% unapologetically.

FUCK WAITING FOR PERMISSION. IT'S GO-TIME!

Remember, back in Chapter 6, how I invited you to own the fact that you're where you are today because of all the choices you've made up until now. That probably felt really confronting because you aren't where you want to be. But the great news was that you're the one who gets to change that, right?

The thing is that it's not enough to know you're responsible for changing things. You have to stop standing on the sidelines, waiting for your life to start. Instead, you have to take inspired action today - otherwise, today becomes tomorrow, tomorrow becomes next year, and next year becomes next decade. You feel me?

The faster you take responsibility for your life and where you are at the moment, the faster things will change. And, sister, there's nothing wrong with today. It's as good a day as any, so why not take even just a tiny step today to get you on that juicy path of yours? Your dream is waiting for you to claim it!

You don't need to wait till January 1ˢᵗ
to set new resolutions.

Most of us have a lot of fun while we're in our 20s. Then suddenly, we hit 30 and we feel like we get an email from the President of the Universe that says, "Sorry, but you now have to grow up. You need to forfeit all those dreams you had. You need to be practical and settle down from this point forward. Oh, and PS? Don't be too fussy."

That's how I felt. Turning 30 terrified me, because I wasn't where I wanted to be at all. In fact, I was living a life that was the polar opposite of where I thought I'd be. It was hard to watch all my friends settling down into their relationships. Meanwhile, I felt stuck waiting for my soulmate to be my savior - my knight in shining armor - who'd make everything OK.

The problem is that life doesn't work like that. Remember: it's never the man who's missing! I'm so clear on this now, but I didn't know it back then. I was too far down the rabbit hole of lack and the feeling that love never happened for me. I was too committed to the idea that 'When he shows up, THEN everything's going to work out'.

So I just waited. I focused on getting ready to be ready. I put off my joy and my happiness. And most of all, I hid from my greater purpose.

I had to get how unhappy I actually was, and how much I was hiding in my life, before I was ready to take responsibility for changing anything. I had to recognize that I wasn't ready for the soulmate relationship I longed for.

Only once I owned that responsibility could the truth set me free.

Only then could it catapult me onto a new path.

IT'S TIME TO LIVE YOUR PURPOSE

I know, I know. That 'p-word' - purpose - is enough to scare many people away. When they hear it, they feel enormous pressure. That's often because they're lazy and content to cruise along in a job they don't even like. Meanwhile, they just wait for purpose to waltz into their lives one day. Or they wait for a guru to dish it out to them on a silver platter.

Some of them drink themselves into oblivion, hoping that one day, that bottle of red wine will just hand them their purpose and they'll suddenly have a big revelation. Or maybe that spiritual retreat they book into will reveal their purpose to them.

But sister, that's just NOT how it works.

Let me break the idea of 'purpose' down for you to make it super-easy for you to digest. Your purpose is nothing more or less than doing what lights you up. If you don't know what that is, the quickest way to get a clue is to look at your life today. For example:

- Look at your bookshelf. What are the books you can't help but buy?
- What do you Google in your spare time when you need a break from reality?
- Who do you follow on social media that has nothing to do with your job or self-development?
- What activities make time stand still for you because you're so in the moment doing them?
- What do you fantasize about?
- If you could do anything, what would you do?
- When you have enough money, what would you love to do?

Ignoring your purpose means letting yourself stagnate without using your gifts. Without purpose in your life, there's no satisfaction, no fulfillment and sure as hell no growth.

I realized just how off-purpose I was during the global financial crisis. So many people were being laid off, and I used the climate to rationalize away my dream. I guarantee you're doing the same thing right now, beauty. I know you are, because every single one of my clients does.

But your heart knows better. That's why you're still reading this book. It's why you just can't settle. You know there's more. A LOT more.

And when you prioritize saying 'yes' to your gifts, I promise you that your soulmate will show up. In fact, focusing on your purpose is the quickest shortcut you can take to attract him.

Do you first, and then watch him show up.

Here's the deal. When you commit to prioritizing your happiness and joy, the Law of Attraction will bring in an amazing man who's ALSO doing what he loves. He'll be drawn to your energy because you're in alignment with your heart, your soul and your inner world.

You'll be happy, in flow and joyful… and that's when you activate your own magnetism and attract everything you desire with ease. It might sound too good to be true, but it's not.
It's simply the way your Vortex works.

SO HOW DO YOU LIVE ON PURPOSE?

If you're from a family of doctors, it'll feel a little odd to suddenly just say, "Hey, I want to go off and be a crystal healer," or, "I want to open a flower shop!" It'll be a little removed from your family's experience, so telling them (or even just thinking about the idea) can be daunting.

But the permission can only come from one person, darling woman, and that's you.

MY MOMENT OF TRUTH

When I finally woke up and realized that I was denying my truth, my purpose and my gifts, I quickly saw that it was costing me everything. I didn't feel healthy or happy. I felt stressed, tired and hungover.

I'd been numbing the fact that I wasn't where I wanted to be for so long that I had no idea how bad it had become. I thought, "Holy shit. There's nothing powerful about my life right now. Am I genuinely OK with spending the next 40 years hiding from the gifts that I know are inside me, and hiding from who I was born to be?"

Luckily, the answer was a resounding, "Fuck, no!"

So the next day, I went to my boss with big sunglasses on because I knew there'd be tears. And I said, "I know you guys keep trying to grow me, and I'm grateful, but this isn't where I'm meant to be." I told him I had no idea what was next, but that I'd been living in a fog for so long and pretending so much that I'd forgotten who I was.

I told him that I was completely off my path and wanted to get back on it. And then I finished by saying, "I'm fully committed to finding out who this amazing woman is, and I'm ready to turn the lights back on and get my sparkle back."

My boss's eyes welled up as he replied, "I'm so proud of you,

Lucy, I know you're not flourishing here, and you've got all these talents that you dabble with from time to time." He was talking about my side gigs singing and auditioning for the odd part, and he was right: I'd only ever dabbled with them up until then.

And it was only once I stopped dabbling and living at about 20% of who I was that I could finally start living on purpose. I was so lucky to have a boss who recognized that and supported me. I walked out, committed to living 100% on purpose from that moment on – and I've never looked back.

Now, I'm not telling you that you've got to do what I did - go straight out and quit your job. Instead, I'm inviting you to admit the truth of how you're showing up for yourself right now in all areas of your life. Remember: if you're reading this book because you're telling yourself, "All I need to do is work out how to attract my soulmate," that simply isn't true.

Close your eyes, put your hands on your heart, check in and let yourself connect with your truth. Are you really where you want to be in your life at the moment? Is what you're doing feeding your soul? Or are you holding back and settling for just enough?
Believe me, the man is just the cherry on top of your beautiful, decadent, six-layer cake. He's just the cherry. Really take that in. *He's just the cherry.*

And you, my darling, are the entire six layers of delicious, decadent cake.

So, stop making it about the man. Start pouring your energy and focus into yourself and your life! Because this will be the fast track to attracting in the love of your life - your soul partner, your kindred spirit, your best friend and your rock.

I've said it before: we attract who we are. So you have to start by getting interested in the woman YOU are and ask yourself, *"What lights me up? What am I passionate about?"* Then you need to put all of your energy into that, instead of hiding behind anxiety and depression, or numbing yourself with Netflix and booze.
Your purpose isn't complicated. It's been in you since the day you were born. It's like your own personal dharma.

Connecting with it is just about getting still, getting conscious and asking yourself, *"What am I going to do with today that would feed my soul?"* And it might be something really, really simple. Maybe you've been wanting to play the piano for over 20 years. If so, go and book a piano lesson. Or if you know how to play, then prioritize time to sit down and practice.

> *Whatever it is, go and do the thing that will bring you back to life.*

DON'T GET STUCK IN PLAN B

Remember Susie, back in Chapter 7? Her Plan B for having babies was to have them by herself. And beauty, I see that all the time. Women tell me, "I want to have children, and I'm fine to have them on my own."

I always reply, "OK, that's cool. It's awesome that in this day and age, you actually can do that. But what do you truly want?"

And 99.99% of the time, they say, "Well... I don't want to have a baby on my own. I just need to keep the door open, because love never works out for me. So, I'm OK with having a baby on my own."

Sister, if you're just 'OK' with something, that means it's your Plan B. And that Plan B is DESTROYING your Plan A.
Energy flows where attention goes, so if you're putting your energy into your Plan B, that's exactly what you'll get. Having a Plan B is another way to give up on your dreams. You might think having a

backup plan is smart. You might think it's the responsible thing to do.

But Plan B puts whatever you're settling for right into your sacred Vortex of creation, and then guess what? You keep attracting the guys who won't commit because you've already given up, and next thing you know, you're living Plan B by default.
So I want you to check in with yourself right this fucking second: is Plan B actually where you want to end up?

Susie finally acknowledged that she didn't want to end up in her Plan B. And once she realized that, she was 100% unapologetic about choosing her Plan A.

When you realize that this one life is all you've got, you'll truly ignite your purpose. You'll walk around every day connected to your heart and your yoni, sending out powerful #vaginavibes into the world.

Look, I thought I'd become a coach when I somehow had my shit together - sometime around age 65, I told myself, when I actually had some wisdom. Then it hit me that I might not ever GET to 65!
I expect to, but what if I didn't? Nothing in this life is guaranteed. And the deeper part of me - the part that knew I had a book to write and women to coach and inspire - stepped up.

When I got out of my own way and connected with all the possibilities, it felt good. I asked myself:

- *"What if I could inspire others right now?"*
- *"What if I could have an impact right now?"*
- *"What if I didn't have to be perfect?"*

That's when things got real. I chose to step up fully into all my glory with my heart wide open, and I said to myself, *"Fuck it, I'm going there! I'm going to take up space, shine my light and share my wisdom. No more holding back. No more playing small. No more trying to fit in with who I 'think' I should be. Look out world, 'cos here I come!"*
And things can get every bit as real for you too. But if you keep just waiting for life to happen to you, you're going to die a sad woman with

a ton of regret, and I know that's not why you're here.

You have talents too. There's a reason you're here, gorgeous. And if you get serious about committing to yourself and creating from your heart, you'll start uncovering who you really are. You'll fall head-over-heels in love with this version of you who trusts herself, backs herself and has a huge light that other people can't wait to bask in.

GOING SIDEWAYS IS A TRAP

Back when I had my revelation, I knew my purpose was acting. But before I'd held the job I was coasting in, I'd been in radio. And initially, I was so out of alignment that when I quit the job, I thought, *"Oh, I'll just get back into radio to start with."*

I've seen the same thing happen with so many women. They'll think they're being uber-courageous and changing their lives when they leave one job... But then they just move sideways into something that's kind of similar, or something they've done before. They move into something that's familiar. They move into something that's not-quite-what-they-ACTUALLY-wanted. They move into something safe.

And safe? Beauty, safe is the enemy of lit.

Safe was what radio was for me.

The problem is that wherever
you go, there you are.

So why do we do this? Deep down, it's because we're scared. We need to feel safe, and we don't trust ourselves or the Universe to have our backs. So we don't acknowledge our truths. We refuse to spend the time in our Vortexes, consciously creating the lives of our dreams.

We don't believe that we can have life exactly the way we want it. We try to tell ourselves that 'good enough is enough'.

Many of my clients are also scared that other people - often parents or friends – won't approve if they do what they truly want to do with their lives. They haven't yet created or claimed their own identities. They haven't found their own voices or figured out how to develop their certainty muscles.

That's exactly what it was like for me. I ended up going out and applying for radio jobs, because I told myself that I couldn't do acting. I told myself I'd missed the boat. I didn't feel excited to get back into radio though, which was a whopping red flag that it wasn't right for me. (Because when something is right, it will seriously excite you.)

Yes, radio was different from being in the corporate world. But it was something I'd already done, and there was a reason I'd left it. What I wanted to do more than anything was to act, but I was telling myself, *"I'm too old now for acting now. If I was going to do it, I'd have done it by now, so obviously I can't do that."*

Instead, I went sideways and applied for all those radio jobs instead. I talked myself out of acting before I even gave it a chance.

Did you hear that? I talked myself out of the one thing that I knew to be true, the one passion I was craving, because I told myself it was too late. That's the biggest crock of shit you can possibly tell yourself, gorgeous woman.
So I want you to look at your life today and see where YOU'RE talking yourself out of that thing that you know in your heart and soul would bring you back to life. And I want you to really hear this:

YOU are the chief architect of your life.
You get to design your life exactly the way you want it.

If you decide to take your power back into your own hands and remember that you need to be your own 'No. 1', everything will start aligning for you. If you don't, you'll live your life as a small version of yourself who's constantly trying to prove yourself to your parents. You'll constantly do what you think you should be doing, and end up living someone else's life.

And if you take that path? You're NOT going to be happy when you get to your deathbed. As you take your last breath, it'll come with a flood of 'I should's and 'I wish I had's. You'll have so many regrets, and I don't want that for you. Deep down, you know YOU don't want that for you either.

I know you're reading this book because you want to attract your soulmate. And in order to actually get on the path to calling him in, you're going to need to give up your Plan B. Surrender it.
You can't have your Plan A while you're making space for Plan B.

LISTEN TO THAT NUDGE
FROM THE UNIVERSE

When I was considering going back into radio, one man helped to change the trajectory of my life with only a few words.

I sent my radio demo to him, and he emailed me some honest feedback. His message said, "Lucy, you've got a fantastic voice. It's a great demo and it's kind of funny. But you need to go and get in touch with your truth. Go and do acting."

I'll never forget that day. I thought, "Who's this guy to tell me that I'm 'kind of funny'?" All the other feedback I'd got had been very, very good. But those four short sentences completely changed my life.

I felt like the Universe was working through another human being to give me that message. Clearly, I hadn't given myself

> *permission to get out there, take a risk and just act. I was
> too busy playing it safe and telling myself that it was too
> late. So my permission needed to come from someone else.*
>
> *After I read his email, I immediately Googled acting courses.
> And ten minutes later, I'd booked myself into a six-week
> course. I didn't even compare different courses — I just
> booked one in. I knew it was the most aligned thing I'd done
> in a long, long time, and it felt damn good.*
>
> *And the rest, as you know, is history.*

BECOME AN EXPERT IN YOUR JOY

I've asked you to check in with yourself a few times in this chapter already, and I want you to do it again right now. Check in and ask yourself where you're hiding or telling yourself that something's not possible.

- Maybe you want to go and live in Turkey, but you have a mortgage. If so, get someone in to rent your apartment, or sell the damn thing.
- Maybe you've always wanted to learn tantric sex, but you don't know where to start and it's not what people in your circle do. If so, screw that (pun totally intended)! Go hit up Google to find a school in your area or an online program, then choose the one that feels best and sign up.
- Maybe you've always wanted to learn Italian and rent a villa in Italy for three months? In that case, Google villas in whichever area you've always wanted to explore, pick a date and ask your boss if you can work remotely. (And if you work for yourself, even better - just grab your laptop and enjoy!)

Whatever your heart is nudging you to do, make that the focus. Give yourself to it and make it a priority. Remember that whenever you honor your heart, you're honoring your truest path. When you do that, everything falls into place. The Universe always gets behind you when you follow your heart. (Also, putting a date on any action is the most powerful thing you can do for yourself - no date, no action.)

None of us need all the stuff we've collected in our lives. Yet we cling to it, and let it stop us from taking action. Remember: we all die. If you actually let that in, it'll help you to be bold and realize that you don't need these material things. What you need, more than any-thing, is to feed your soul. That's what will keep you alive and vital. That's what will make you thrive while you still have the gift of being alive, instead of just existing and living in survival mode.

I realized this when I left my job and took that very first scary, big, bold risk. That was the beginning of my new path.

I made joy my new obsession.

Joy was the one thing I committed to. For the first time in my life, I stopped caring what my friends thought of me and my decisions. I stopped caring about what my family thought I should be doing. I'd been denying myself my own happiness for way too long, so I made a sacred vow to myself that I'd only listen to my heart when I made decisions from then on. I vowed that I'd put myself first in all areas, no matter what.

And now, I invite you to do the same thing. I invite you to step up and start fighting for what you want. Stop letting yourself off the hook be-cause you've got some fancy backup Plan B that you're now stuck in.

When you make joy your new obsession, you don't wait for the week-end to experience it. Instead, you find ways to sprinkle it throughout your week. And when you do this, you'll be so freaking happy, which - to me - is what real success is.

But to do this, you have to get out of your comfort zone. You have to start getting creative and connecting with your feelings and truth.

You have to dedicate time to consciously hanging out in your Vortex each day, connecting with your heart and really feeling what it's like to have your dream life, RIGHT NOW.

Remember that every time you do this, you recalibrate your cells to vibrate with this reality as if it's already happened. And when you do THAT, the Law of Attraction will set it up for you. You just have to keep strengthening your belief and imagination muscles by making this your first-thing-in-the-morning and last-thing-at-night rituals.

Do this, and watch the magic unfold.

Is there a career shift that you've been putting off? A hobby you'd like to try that you've not made time for? Somewhere you'd like to travel?

Like I said, I'm not telling you that you have to quit your job. Just go and try things that you think you might enjoy. Life won't just make a 'purpose manual' appear in your lap one day.

Life either happens to you, or it happens for you, and those are two very different worlds. So don't wait for something cataclysmic to take place. Don't wait for disease or cancer to wake you up. Don't be lazy and let life happen to you. Start being an advocate for yourself and step into becoming the woman that you were born to be.

Get out of your comfort zone. **It's time to get uncomfortable.**

At the end of the day, coming home to the magic of who you are means making a decision to show up in the world as who you truly are. It means putting your energy into your gifts and the things that make you happy. And yes, it's clichéd to 'do the things that make you happy'. But sister, doing anything else will kill your dreams and your mojo.

And is that seriously the way you want to live?

CHANGING YOUR LIFE IS AN INSIDE JOB

I want you to give yourself permission this instant to be your epic, glorious self. It's possible that, up until now, no one's ever given you that permission. If so, you've probably been living according to what your mum or dad wanted for you, or who you think you *should* be in your society or culture.

And I want you to decide that living that way ends in THIS moment. Decide that it's your birthright to be happy and have love in your life. Decide that you owe it to yourself to start speaking up, to take up space, and to stop giving your energy and your power away to what other people think.

When I had my corporate job, I was a square peg trying to fit into a round hole. I was pretending and trying to fit into who I thought I should be. To stop that, I had to take responsibility for standing on my own two feet and living my life in a way that felt true for me.

Like I've said before, taking that responsibility won't be comfortable - but it will be totally worth it! The process will be messy. You'll need to be an archeologist, digging up all the repressed rage in the ancient ruins of your deepest self. And you'll need to be patient with the process. You'll also need to be courageous and back yourself the whole way.

Because, yeah sure, you can stay comfortable - but staying comfortable means no change. You'll never uncover the buried treasure in those ancient ruins if you aren't willing to get messy.

YOU HAVE TO BE READY

When Heidi first came to me, she was so shut-down that she couldn't even connect to the questions I asked her. Her coping mechanism was laughter, and the deeper my questions got, the more she laughed.

She didn't realize this was a coping mechanism. She had no idea that laughing allowed her to subconsciously shrug off her pain. I had to send her away multiple times until she could actually drop into her heart and feel the questions I was asking her.

By the time I invited Heidi in, she was genuinely ready. Her armor was down. She'd disarmed her coping mechanisms, and she was finally excited to jump in with both feet.

She was ready to commit like a superstar, and her commitment inspired all the women in the community. Then, when she got the first glimpse of her true power, she could see how apologetic she'd been her entire life in every area, which – of course – was really confronting. She realized it all stemmed from not having been emotionally supported as a little girl.

This massive AHA moment unearthed Heidi's thirst to unapologetically blaze a new path where she gets to create, reframe and rebuild every part of her life the way she wants it to be. She's now a Queen on a mission, and is fully empowered and embodied in who she is.

Now, when challenges come up for her, she gets excited and sees them as opportunities for growth and power. In other words, she knows how to reframe the fuck out of them.

And most importantly, she's proud of – and in love with – her new, unapologetic self.

Anything that offers the chance to up-level your life will include leaving the familiar path and jumping on 'the path less traveled'. I'm pretty sure you're not reading this book because you want things to stay the same, so you're going to need to leap out of your comfort zone. You'll need to start putting yourself out there and living with an open heart.

Opportunities will present themselves when you're open to receiving them. Fear will come up too, but if there's excitement mixed in with the fear, you can trust that it's a good decision and a risk worth taking.

I'm actually addicted to taking risks now, as long as they feel right. I don't overthink my decisions any more like I used to. If something feels right, I know it's my answer. Of course, fear still comes up for me - but I know the difference between 'fear because something isn't right' and 'fear that's mixed with adrenaline and OMG I'm doing this!'

And I always know that when I leap into the unknown with that giddy, excited fear, gold is going to follow. I've said it before, but the Universe really does favor the bold! Sitting in your comfort zone is predictable, and it's not giving you anything but a flat pancake butt. The fact that you're reading this book means that you're far from predictable, so it's time to kick that comfortable habit, stat!

YOU DON'T HAVE TO DO IT ALONE

I learned that the quickest way to step up was to find the right support. To find a sisterhood who all wanted to be the best versions of themselves too. Being part of that collective energy is the quickest way to rise. It's so powerful and potent.

Women come into the Vortex that I've created, and within a single day, they message me saying, "Oh my God, Lucy. It's safe to be me. I can feel myself for the first time." And they see themselves in the other women around them who are also fighting for their dreams. The women who also want to be the best versions of themselves.
They feel liberated and know deep in their hearts that this sisterhood will change their lives.

Remember: we're all the sum of the five people that we spend the most time with. And that means you've got to start getting very deliberate about who you're living your life with. You need to ask yourself, *"Are these friendships serving me, or am I just over-giving and depleting myself?"*

And if your answer is the second option, divine woman, you've got to tighten up your boundaries and start choosing you in every moment.

Once again, you HAVE to put yourself first. You've got to prioritize loving yourself if you expect someone else to love you. You've got to invest time in yourself if you expect a man to come and invest time in you.

That's just the way that it works.

DON'T wait to be rescued. Don't wait for life to just suddenly present you with the path you should be on. And stop looking for yourself, too! You're right here, right now, with gifts inside of you.

All you've got to do is allow yourself to connect with your truth and ask:

- *"What if I did know what I loved?"*
- *"What if I did know what my passion was?"*
- *"What if I got out of the story that I didn't know either of those things?"*

And then every day, tell the Universe, "I'm going to let my passion come to me today. Hey, Universe, what would you have me do right now?"

That's what I invite you to do in this moment. One step at a time, let the truth in. Let it in. Let it affect you.

Start living your unapologetic life.

THE GOLD NUGGETS

Beautiful woman, we've covered some gold together in the last few pages. Here's a quick recap of the 24-karat nuggets to take away with you and treasure as you head into the next chapter:

- You have to stop living life apologetically, and start having a deep reverence for your own power and majesty.

- Living apologetically can look like waiting for permission, waiting to be saved or settling for Plan B.

- Purpose is the antidote to settling, and finding your purpose is your fast track to finding your soulmate.

- Become the world's leading expert in what brings you joy, and your purpose will follow.

- Plug into your courage, back yourself, explore your gifts, put your energy into what turns you on, and above all, BE UNAPOLOGETIC about it!

GIFT WORK

Over to you, superstar! Take these final actions and really feel the Universe align with your dreams. Take out your journal and give yourself the time to go deep into your heart and your desires. Then ask yourself:

- What is it that you're not giving yourself permission to follow through on?

- What grabs your attention?
- What do you spend time Googling in those moments when you go into autopilot? What are the topics?
- What is it that your heart wants to do? Is it interior design? Is it acting? Would you secretly love to be a celebrant or a wedding planner?

Now close your eyes, and put your right hand on your heart and your left hand on your beautiful belly. Yes, you know the drill. Connect with whatever it is that you actually want, divine woman. Then ask yourself:

- Where would you love to be six months from now?
- How about a year from now?
- What would you love to be celebrating?
- How would you truly love to feel in your body?

It's so easy to forget (I know I forgot) that we have a choice 24/7. Every moment is a gift, and you've got to get intentional. You have to put a deadline on the things that you keep saying you'll do one day 'when you have time' or 'when you have enough money or knowledge'

Finally, remember to say and feel your affirmations daily. Shut that victimhood down by choosing the affirmations that you need in the moment. Give the ones below a whirl and see if they feel good for you:

- "I am enough."
- "I am worthy."
- "I am whole."
- "I have a passion."
- "I have a purpose."
- "I am lovable."
- "The Universe co-creates with me every single day."
- "I am supported."
- "I am loved."
- "I am valuable."

- "I'm here to make a difference."
- "I'm going to let myself feel joy right now."

I'M DONE.

Beautiful woman, this book has been one epic download! And now, at the end of it, I want to remind you that YOU — my stunning, divine, extraordinary, talented woman — are the creator of your life.

I've given you the keys to the kingdom, and I'm counting on you to use them. You call the shots from here on in. You get to create and have your life the way you want it.

There is absolutely nothing wrong with you. It's just your belief system and identity that need an overhaul. And you can have a soulmate relationship as easily as you can manifest a cup of coffee.

We talked about this back in Chapter 10. I told you then that it's as easy to manifest a free cup of coffee as it is to manifest your soulmate. I use this analogy a lot with my women and they frickin' love it. Now, I know what you're thinking... *"That's hilarious, Lucy. If only it were that easy! I'm good with the coffee bit, but it's harder with the soulmate."*

And you know what? That's because you believe that attracting a cup of coffee is small, easy and do-able, but attracting your soulmate is big, scary and way too hard.

So let's take care of this right now, shall we? I want you to integrate a new, rockstar belief into your cells here and now that will do all the heavy lifting for you. Close your eyes and breathe this belief into your ovaries:

'Attracting my soulmate is as easy as attracting a free cup of coffee.

I do this with ease and so much joy. It's just who I am. I always get what I ask for.'

A belief is just a thought that you give meaning to and then think over and over again. So if you're going to create a belief, make it powerful AF. Then stick to it, put it to work and watch what happens.

I know you know by now that the reason your King hasn't shown up yet is that you've been addicted to thinking the wrong, shitty beliefs over and over again. Those beliefs aren't serving you or working on your behalf. In fact, those thoughts suck balls, and they've been keeping you small and single. Meanwhile, who you really are is an expansive, worthy, incredible woman.

And sister, now it's time to embody that truth! It's time to step into your kingdom of plenty.

Once you sit down and prioritize committing to this book, to the gift work and to yourself, you'll start to shed all the shitty beliefs - piece by piece and layer by layer. You'll open up to actually being able to let this in fully. You'll start to feel so fucking unstoppable, and it will change your life in ways you can't even fathom in this moment.

Trust me: if I can go from sucking at love and being the queen of sabotage with a Masters in people-pleasing to being married to the love of my life and a mum to the most incredible baby girl, then gorgeous woman, you definitely can too. **Because you get to have life the way you want it.**

When resistance comes up (and it will), just high-five it and know that it's normal. Know that you're on the right track and that Rome wasn't built in a day. Keep taking one step at a time, ENJOY the process, and have fun as it unfolds. Enjoy the many, many AHA moments that come your way too. Prioritize JOY every day, and also... grow a bit of patience, because being needy looks shit on you.

Embrace all the twists and turns. Lean into them, and celebrate the fuck out of all your shit coming up. It only comes up because it's begging to be cleared, so you can create the most epic Vortex to attract from.

You, my darling, were born for greatness. You are fucking extraordinary. You are an amazing woman with a powerful story inside of you. Don't let anyone tell you that your dream is too big or that you're too much. Rise into all that you were born to be. Claim your spot at the table and expand into the brilliance of your limitless soul. Get that sparkle back into your eyes so you can magnetize your desires right now.

This is your golden opportunity.

Thank you for letting me in, and for trusting me with your beautiful heart and truth. You truly are a rockstar for reading this cover to cover. I'm sure there were moments that you wanted to jump ship and tell me to take a hike, but you didn't.
So don't stop now. You're just getting started and this is the beginning of the rest of your life. You are a Queen now, and Queens sit in their knowing with full faith that their every wish gets granted.

You deserve the world, but remember: we don't get what we deserve. We get what we expect, so start expecting miracles on tap, orgasms, Mr Right, aligned opportunities, epic health and a smoking hot bank account.

Go shine your incredible, radiant light and be unapologetically YOU. Keep those boundaries strong. They expand you and keep you moving smoothly down your dream highway so you can allow everything you've ever wanted into your life.

Step up, show up, back yourself, ask for what you want and don't look back.

And keep in mind that you don't have to do this alone. This doesn't have to be goodbye. If you want more, come and say hello in my free Facebook group - Ignite Your Queen Attract Your Soulmate.

Find us at _www.facebook.com/groups/IgniteYourQueen_, click 'Join', and you'll become part of a super-supportive sisterhood of women who are ready to open their hearts and turn up their lights. They're also on their path to attracting their soulmates, and they'll hold you accountable to your dreams.

One final reminder, divine one: good things don't come to those who wait. Good things come to those who ask.

So don't let anyone shit in your Vortex, and for God's sake, don't shit in your own!

Love you xx

I'M DONE.

Dream highway

When you're aligned and in flow, it's like you're on a 'dream highway' that takes you to your dream.

To stay on course on this highway, you must do what lights you up and inspires you. You must stay true to what makes you happy. Following your passion will keep you flying down the dream highway.

Get onto your dream highway by hanging out in your Vortex and feeling how wonderful your life is today. Then stay on it by being discerning about who you allow as your passengers.

Flow

When you're living fully aligned with your inner life and your heart, and you let go of control and instead trust in the unfolding, you're in the flow zone.

When this happens, the right events and people effortlessly appear in your life. You might feel like this could just be a string of amazing coincidences, but it's not.

It's flow. You experience this because you've taken your foot off the brakes, and have started allowing all the magic to unfold in your life without trying to make things happen.

Little girl

(AKA 'inner little girl')

At different ages in your childhood, you have unpleasant experiences that you don't know how to process or deal with. These experiences make you subconsciously decide that, to stay safe, you'll never let that type of experience happen to you ever again.

Your inner 'little girl' is the part of you that never moved beyond that experience. You can have many different little girls inside you - each of them stuck at the age when you had the unpleasant experience. And when something happens in your adult life that reminds your little girl of that experience, she'll hop behind the steering wheel of your life and take control to try to protect you.

Embracing each little girl, loving on them and supporting them is a pivotal part of the process of stepping into your Queen self. These little girls hold the keys to everything you desire, so I'm excited for you to take each of them under your wing from this moment on and to love on them every day like you would a newborn baby.

Rage Pages

Underneath your inner little girls lies a lot of anger, hurt and rage that they either weren't allowed or were too scared to express in the moment you had the experience. This anger and rage was locked deep down inside of you, and it needs to be felt in order to be released and healed.

Rage Pages (also known as Power Pages) are journal pages that allow you to privately, freely express all those stifled emotions. When you write your Rage Pages, you can swear away and rage your heart out at anyone and anything. You can express all the things you've always wanted to say but couldn't.

I recommend safely disposing of your Rage Pages once you've finished raging. Burn the pages (safely, of course) and then have a good dance-off to shift the toxic energy once you've released it from your cells. It's time to let it all go, beauty!

Reframe

If you're feeling stuck, looking at a situation from a different perspective will help to shift you back into alignment.

'Reframing' means choosing a positive new perspective (frame) to view a previously negative experience or obstacle through.

Shitsville

This is a proverbial village where everything's out of alignment, and everyone prefers to claim that their life is out of their control. This is a place where your word has no value and your self-worth is near zero. When you've given up and / or are settling, you're out of alignment with your flow and you're in Shitsville (also known as 'Victim Village').

Vortex

This is your infinite well of creation. It exists whether you're aware of it or not. However, if you consciously connect with it, spend time in it and take care of it, you can create anything in your life that you desire.

Visualize your Vortex any way you like. I see mine as an infinite, expansive ocean of possibility that I get to fill with whatever I choose.

Vulnerability

Vulnerability is your secret superpower! When you're truly vulnerable, you're acting from an open heart and you have the courage to express how you really feel. You let people see the real you and your imperfections. You stand in your full, glorious, feminine power.

True vulnerability requires you to own your desires and be unapologetic about them. It's about speaking your truth and not giving a fuck whether people can handle it. Do this, and watch your life transform epically!

Vibration

At the subatomic level, everything and everyone is made up of energy that's constantly vibrating. We live in a vibrational universe.

Our feelings and beliefs create the world around us by changing our vibration. Feelings and beliefs live within the heart space. When what we express aligns with our feelings and beliefs, we can consciously create our lives. When what we express betrays our feelings and beliefs, we lose that ability.

We're vibrating at all times - both with what we want and what we don't want. Oftentimes, we say we want something, but deep inside we're vibrating with NOT wanting it. The Law of Attraction responds to the strongest vibration, which is often the not wanting. That's why so many people can't create the life they desire.

To create the life of your dreams, get busy feeling all of your desires fully so you change your vibration.

Printed in Great Britain
by Amazon

79914662R00182